FLESH

"Scarcely a mome
from his place of c
to the mystery of the sound. From the edge of the
Woodlands there appeared a hideous head upon a
swaying neck at least 20 feet in length. The head was
that of a wolf or dog, save that there was a
prolongation into a huge bill or horny jaws. This bill
the monster opened at intervals, displaying a row of
immense fangs upon each division, while as he
opened it up on each occasion was admitted a
hissing noise loud enough to be heard for a great
distance. From the back of his head and down the
neck descended a mane of coarse reddish hair. The
monster retained its position for a moment or two,
swaying its head gently back and forth, when its eyes
fell upon the bull; then it at once showed signs of
great excitement. It snorted fiercely, the hissing
sound became almost continuous, and it would
repeatedly open its immense jaws and snap them
together with a sound like the report of a rifle. Its
hesitation did not long continue. Maddened by the
sight of the bull, the monster advanced at once and
swiftly to the attack. Raising its head still higher it
shot forward over the fence, and thence came over
in swift, billowing undulations, the fence seeming no
obstacle at all. As the animal entered the field its
whole body could be distinctly seen. The great neck
terminated in a body of somewhat less length,
supported upon four short legs, armed with
immense claws, though the motions of the animal
seemed to resemble rather those of a snake than of
a thing with legs."

THE DIABOLUS MARIS.

SOUTHERNERS & SAURIANS

Swamp Monsters, Lizard Men,
and Other Curious Creatures
of the Old South

By John LeMay

Bicep Books
Roswell, NM

First Edition

LeMay, John.
    Southerners and Saurians:
    Swamp Monsters, Lizard Men, and Other Curious Creatures
of the Old South
        1. History—Old South. 2. Cryptozoology/Remnant dinosaurs.
3. Folklore.

FOR MY FAVORITE SKEPTIC,
JUSTIN MULLIS

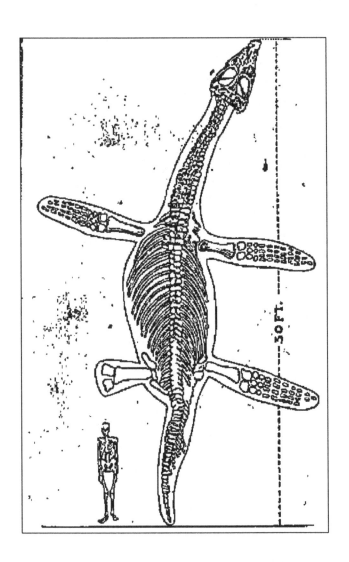

30 FT.

PREFACE

Considering that the last two books in this series explored dinosaur/cryptid sightings during the Old West period, I thought it would be interesting to explore the mysterious creatures of the Old South. Actually, several of the chapters in this book were initially intended for *Cowboys & Saurians: Dinosaurs and Prehistoric Beasts as Seen by the Pioneers.* At the time of that book's writing, I wasn't aware of just how many alleged dinosaur sightings that the Old West had. It soon became apparent to me that if I included them all, the book would get out of hand.

As my digging through old newspaper articles progressed, I found quite a few interesting stories centering on or taking place in the Southern part of the United States. These tales were distinctly different from their Western counterparts, often being set in a swampy marshland that didn't exactly mesh with the pioneer/western angle of the first book.

Slowly, I began to file them away as work progressed on the first book. Afterall, I was already filing away newspaper reports on Ice Age megafauna for a second book, *Cowboys & Saurians: Ice Age.* It was my hope that enough articles would be unearthed to do a third book with an eye towards the South. Thankfully, there were, and that is how *Southerners & Saurians: Swamp Monsters, Lizard Men, and Other Curious Creatures of the Old South* came to be!

I hope you enjoy it.

THE AUTHOR

JOHN P. LEMAY
Roswell, New Mexico.
April, 2020.

CONTENTS

INTRODUCTION   11

CHAPTERS

LIST OF ILLUSTRATIONS

INTRODUCTION:
CRYPTIDS OF THE CIVIL WAR

There's some interesting parallels between the Old West and the Old South. For starters, there's the historical influence of the Civil War, which raged from 1861 to 1865. One could argue that the death of the Old South gave life to the Old West. As it is, the Old South is the collective term for the pre-Civil War South, which naturally came to an end when slavery was abolished after the war. Seven hundred fifty thousand people died during the conflict between the Confederate and Union armies, and the South was mostly in ruins once it ended. Again, hence the term Old South. It was the very year that the war ended, 1865, that historians also consider to be the start of the Wild West/Old West period of U.S. history. In that sense, the Old West and Old South are irrevocably tied.

Southerners & Saurians

However, in many respects, the Old West and the Old South are polar opposites of one another. This is evidenced by what the public has chosen to romanticize about them over the years. Whereas the West had its cowboys and saloon girls, the South had its "southern gentlemen" and "southern belles." Architecturally speaking, the Old South was defined by monolithic state capitals and elaborate plantations lined with trees. Again, the exact opposite, the Old West was often visualized in the form of a dusty dirt street lined with saloons and bawdy houses. The biggest difference between the two is how they are defined geographically. The Old West is associated with vast stretches of prairie and dry deserts, while the South is characterized by its wet, murky green swampland.

And beneath the placid waters of those swamps hides a multitude of monsters, familiar and new. Armchair cryptozoologists will recognize the usual suspects of pterosaurs and plesiosaurs. Newer, and stranger, are the not so usual suspects: the Lizard-men, the Crocodingo, the Wog, Skunk Apes, giant mosquitos and leeches... As you can see, in the Old South, even the cryptids were different.

And though we've been discussing the pre-Civil War South, it should be noted that, in terms of newspaper reports, Southern cryptids weren't spotlighted until after the Civil War. Naturally, at the time, reporters had more pressing matters to write about than Bigfoot (or "Wild Men" as they were known back then). But Bigfoot and his cryptid brethren did make appearances during the Civil War. Some even say that the cryptids took sides in the conflict, though this is likely just folklore. But like many legends, it may have roots in the truth.

THE WHITE RIVER MONSTER C.1970s.

The White River Monster, if reports are true, could be considered a Union hero. Though the monster didn't come to prominence until sightings in the early 20th Century, folklore claimed that the monster took part in the Civil War. Specifically, it was rumored that the monster was responsible for overturning a Confederate gunboat in Arkansas' White River. Further stories say that it overturned other boats in the river, and yet another story had soldiers shooting at it from the riverbanks.

However, even though there is substantial evidence to support the White River Monster's existence, including a photo from the 1970s, even the monster's supporters admit there's a possibility these stories were concocted after the creature entered the public eye. So bottom line, yes, there probably is a White River Monster of some kind, but its participation in the Civil War is dubious.

Then there are incidents surrounding the Battle of Chickamauga in southeastern Tennessee and northwestern Georgia. The battle, which raged from September 19–20, 1863, is ranked by many as second only to Gettysburg in terms of its body count.

THE BATTLE OF CHICKAMAUGA.

Lore has it that the battle was preceded by a bad omen. The night before the fight began, two Tennessee infantrymen supposedly heard an unearthly shriek while on picket duty. The duo crept to the edge of the woods from where the sound emanated and glimpsed a hairy, ten-foot-tall monster. Its eyes radiated like hot coals and it smelt of rotten meat. When the soldiers ran back to camp to tell their superiors of the wicked vision they had beheld, no one believed them. The next morning, a sergeant went to the spot where they saw the creature and found 22-inch footprints in the earth.

Bigfoot wasn't the only strange entity associated with the battle. Also glimpsed was a cryptid later dubbed "Green Eyes." The being was supposedly seen during the aftermath of the battle feeding upon the dead. According to lore, it was humanoid in form, but with great jaws of fanged teeth. It also had glowing green eyes that struck terror into those who saw it. The creature is seen off and on to this day, but seems to have more in common with paranormal specters rather than flesh and blood cryptids.

On that note, there are plenty of other strange detours we could take into the Civil War, ranging from divine visions of George Washington to the appearance of alien beings. But this isn't a book about ghosts or extraterrestrials; it's about the prehistoric saurians and their brethren. Saurians, for those unaware, is a by now antiquated term that refers to any reptilian creature that resembles lizards, be it prehistoric or otherwise. I was very careful when choosing that title for the first book so that I wouldn't be limited solely to dinosaurs.

In fact, you won't find a great many traditional dinosaurs in this book. What you'll find is much, much stranger, which is another reason this tome stands apart from its two predecessors. So, prepare to enter a realm consisting not only of dinosaurs, but also flying snakes, lizardmen, frog people,

Southerners & Saurians

Averasboro Gallinippers, and wogs that are distinctly "Southern"...

CHAPTER 1
ALLIGATOR MAN OF PALMETTO CREEK
"An Uncanny Monster."

On June 29, 1988, at 2 A.M., seventeen-year-old Christopher Davis was driving on a lonely road along the Scape Ore Swamp of South Carolina. Just like a scene in a horror movie, he got a flat tire, necessitating that he brave the spooky night air to change it. As soon as he was done fixing it, he began to hear heavy footfalls behind him. He turned to look towards the source of the noise and saw a seven-foot-tall monster. This is what he later told reporters about the incident:

> I looked back and saw something running across the field towards me. It was about 25 yards away and I saw red eyes glowing. I ran into the car and as I locked it, the thing grabbed the door handle. I could see him from the neck

down – the three big fingers, long black nails and green rough skin. It was strong and angry. I looked in my mirror and saw a blur of green running. I could see his toes and then he jumped on the roof of my car. I thought I heard a grunt and then I could see his fingers through the front windshield, where they curled around on the roof. I sped up and swerved to shake the creature off."

Christopher Davis recounts experience with alleged seven-foot tall lizard
Davis shows site off Browntown Road where he says he was attacked

Bumps in the night?

Lee County seeks 'lizard' with bad attitude

By GEORGE GEORGAS
ITEM Staff Writer

*ORIGINAL NEWSPAPER
ACCOUNT C.1988.*

When Davis slammed on his brakes, what would later be dubbed the Lizard Man tumbled to the pavement, allowing Davis to make his escape.

When Davis told his story to the press, it became a nationwide sensation, and not without good reason. Though he couldn't necessarily prove that he saw the Lizard Man, his car had bad scratch marks on the roof, and one of the side mirrors was damaged.

SCAPE ORE SWAMP.
U.S. GEOLOGICAL SURVEY.

On top of that, two other men claimed to have seen the same creature two weeks before, Going back a little further, a sighting was also recorded in the fall months of 1987 by George Holliman Jr.

But, it was Davis's sighting that begat an all-out media frenzy over the Lizard Man (Davis was even invited to be a guest on *The Oprah Winfrey Show*). Naturally, there were plenty of people who doubted Davis's wild tale. Ben Radford, of *The Skeptical Inquirer*, investigated the case with close scrutiny and noted that Davis often changed the details of his ordeal in interviews (however, this is not necessarily uncommon among witnesses remembering traumatic events). He also noted that no photographic evidence ever surfaced of Davis's damaged car. And, though Davis had taken a lie detector test and passed, Radford theorized that might have been a staged publicity stunt.

Interestingly, a similar reptilian sighting took place in the same state in the late 1800s (though this would have been a major asset to the Lizard Man's credibility, it would seem the world had forgotten about the story). One hundred sixty-four miles south of Scape Ore Swamp is Palmetto, South Carolina. On August 10, 1892, the California *Woodland Daily Democrat* reported on what was essentially the same creature, only two feet taller and sporting some fin-like appendages.

An Uncanny Monster

The people residing along Palmetto creek ... as well as those for miles back in the slashes,' are highly excited over the appearance of a strange and uncouth creature in that vicinity. The beast is described as being a creature that far outdoes the nightmare ideas of the mythologists. It is equally at home in the water, on the land or among the tall trees of the neighborhood, where it has been most frequently seen. The general contour of the head reminds one of a gigantic serpent with this exception: The 'snout' terminates in a bulbus [sic], monkey faced knot, which much resembles the physiognomy of some gigantic ape. From the neck down, with

the exception of some fin shaped flippers,
which extend from the arms to the waist, the
creature resembles a man, only that the toes and
fingers are armed with claws from two to six
inches long.

Tracks made by the beast in the soft mud
around Hennis lake have been taken to
Donners Grove, where they are kept on
exhibition in a druggists showcase. Those who
have seen the horn'd thing face to face say that
it is a full nine feet in height, which could hardly
be believed only for the fact that the tracks
mentioned above are within a small fraction of
fifteen inches in length. Fishermen who
surprised the monster sitting silently on a mass
of driftwood declared that its back looked like
an alligator's, and that it had a caudal
termination[1] a yard long, which forked like the
tail of a fish.

That the tracks of the alleged nine-foot-tall
animal measured 15 inches is encouraging because
in 1988, tracks were also found of the seven-foot
Lizard Man, which measured roughly the same
size at 14 inches![2] The 1988 prints were three-toed,

---

[1] This is just a fancy term for tail, by the way.
[2] Approximately two weeks after Davis's sighting, the
Bishopville Sheriff's Department made plaster casts of the
tracks. South Carolina Marine Resources Department
spokesperson Johnny Evans made a statement that the tracks
neither matched, nor could be mistaken for, the footprints of
any recorded animal.

and it's a shame that the 1892 article didn't mention how many claws or digits their tracks had.

And again, I want to reiterate that the 1892 article was largely forgotten and was never brought up once (that I know of) during the 1988 media frenzy. Or, in other words, the 1892 Alligator Man was a forgotten "one-off" cryptid that never gained any popularity in South Carolina folklore. So the witnesses of the late 1980s were certainly not trying to breathe life into an old legend, as they most likely didn't know about it to begin with.

But, couldn't it all be coincidence, you ask? Maybe Davis faked his sighting, and the 1892 story was run of the mill "yellow journalism"? Here's what I have to say about that. If it were a made-up story, then why not just make up a creature with a man's body but an alligator's head? That would seem more along the lines of a newspaper hoax in 1892. The key detail is in this quote, "The general contour of the head reminds one of a gigantic serpent with this exception: The 'snout' terminates in a bulbus [sic], monkey faced knot, which much resembles the physiognomy of some gigantic ape." This lines up much too well with similar lizard man sightings from other locations.

You see, Lizardmen aren't native to South Carolina alone. Ohio, West Virginia, Kentucky, New Jersey, and even Canada have had sightings reported of similar creatures. Then there's the Intulo of South Africa, the Cherufe Lizard Man of South America, the Nagas of India, and the mythical Kappas of Japan.

There are several theories for what these Lizard-men could be, including an alien race known as the Reptilians. Alternatively called reptoids, lizard people, and Draconians, the creatures basically resemble human beings, but are covered in scales and have claws, sharp teeth, and in some cases, tails. Both of the Lizardmen sighted in South Carolina could certainly pass for Reptilians.

But, if aliens are too far out for you, there is another theory, this one of the remnant dinosaurs variety. This particular theory postulates that the creatures aren't traditional prehistoric survivors so much as they are highly evolved dinosaurs.

In 1982, the curator of vertebrate fossils at the National Museum of Canada in Ottawa, Dale A. Russell, put forth an interesting hypothesis that had certain types of dinosaurs not gone extinct, they may have evolved into a more humanoid form. This humanoid form he envisioned looked exactly like a Reptilian, and Russell called it the Dinosauroid.

THE TROODON.

Specifically, Russell proposed that a dinosaur called the Troodon could have evolved into something more akin to a human. His reasoning for this was that the Troodon had an encephalization quotient—or EQ—six times higher than normal dinosaurs. Or, in simpler terms, it had a bigger brain than other dinosaurs in its size class, meaning it had a higher capacity for intelligence.

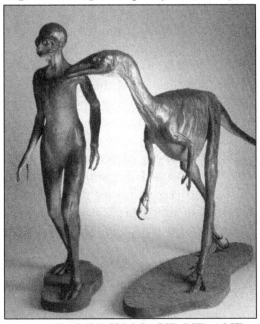

MODEL OF DINOSAUROID AND TROODON.

Russell believed that if the trend in Troodon evolution had continued to the present, its brain case could by now be comparable to that of a human's. Russell also pointed out that Troodontids had good use of the digits on their forelimbs for grasping and manipulation of objects. Notably, the Troodon had three fingers, just like the 1988 Lizard Man...

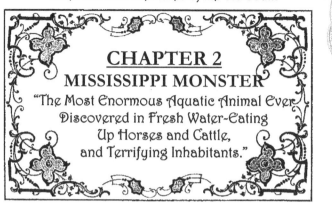

CHAPTER 2
MISSISSIPPI MONSTER
"The Most Enormous Aquatic Animal Ever
Discovered in Fresh Water-Eating
Up Horses and Cattle,
and Terrifying Inhabitants."

O ur next tale takes us to Missouri in the conflux of the Mississippi River. Yes, the same portion of the Mississippi featured in Mark Twain's classic Tom Sawyer and Huck Finn novels. And surely Huck and Tom would have been thrilled to hear of the monster sighted in the river throughout 1877. The first account that I found was published in the *St. Louis Globe-Democrat* on August 29, 1877.

An Aquatic Monster.

The men working at the Government dike in the Mississippi River, opposite Quarantine Station, tell a very curious story concerning a singular monster seen in the water at that point

Southerners & Saurians

on the 6th inst. The reporter's information in the case is Mr. Thomas Eagan one of the workmen alluded to, who lives at 2525 South Seventh street, in this city, who was himself the first to discover this strange aquatic animal, and to call the attention of his fellow-laborers to it. It was about 10 o'clock in the morning, and the day so clear and bright that there could be no optical illusion resulting from any unusual condition of the atmosphere.

Mr. Eagan states that his attention was first directed to a peculiar movement of the water about forty feet above where he was working on the dike. The motion seemed to be caused by a round body rolling over and over in the water with considerable violence, throwing the waves a foot high with each revolution. The object rolled in this manner until it reached a point immediately opposite Eagan and his fellow-workmen, and here it seemed to pause for breath, though at no time being perfectly still. It remained comparatively quiet, however, long enough for the men to get a good sight of part of its body, though it was plain that not more than one-third of its length could be seen. There was about ten feet of the middle portion of the body partly lifted above the water, and though the head was visible several times, the tail was not seen at all, and thus no accurate estimate of the entire length could be made.

The back of the monster was covered with coarse black or dark brown scales, much like those of the alligator, while the under portion of the body, brought frequently to view as the monster turned over, was observed to be of a dark blue, and bright and glistening like that of the Mississippi catfish. The head, most curious to relate, was that of a dog, the ears and eyes being plainly discernible, while the mouth or bill was in the perfect shape of a pelican's, and more than a foot in length. Some of the men who got a good look at the head and ears declare that they were covered with a thick coating of hair, black in color, and hanging down in long, stringy locks. The ears were long and pendant like those of a hound or sea-lion, and several fins. The monster shook them as if to rid his head of the dripping water. From the long bill he threw a stream of water, at intervals, much like the spouting of a whale, and with a noise that was heard by all on shore. The spouts of water were thrown at least two feet high, about a minute apart.

The reptile had either six legs, or four legs and two huge leg-like fins. At any rate two of these members were much longer and larger than the other four, and were thrown out of and along the surface of the water as if they were being used as paddles for propelling, or keeping the body still, or turning it over. On the thick, corrugated neck there was a long, black mane, roached like that of a horse, and reaching so far down that the ends were lost in the water. Why the monster paused so long opposite the dike cannot be surmised, but it is believed to have been attracted by the noise and shouting of the men at work, for several times it was observed to turn its head in that direction, as if curious to know the cause of so much commotion. One of the men went to a neighboring house for a gun, but a few moments before he returned the monster turned over several times with great velocity, spouted violently, and sunk in the water.

The event created a decided sensation among the large number of workmen engaged in work on the river front, and there was no end to the surmises concerning the real nature of the strange sight. Several contended that it was a sea-serpent, others that it was nothing more than a huge alligator, and others (of a superstitious turn of mind) that it was nothing less than the devil, who had assumed this monstrous guise for some portentous or premonitory purpose. An equal diversity of opinion was held concerning the shape, size, and length of the monster. Some thought it was forty, others sixty, feet in length, and one or two were certain its body was as large as a hogshead, and undoubtedly 100 feet in length. Mr. Eagan's judgement is, and he is doubtless correct, that its length would not exceed thirty feet.

The monster soon returned and was reported on again in the *Chippewa Falls Herald* on September 14, 1877.

A RIVER MONSTER
The Most Enormous Aquatic Animal Ever

Discovered in Fresh Water-Eating Up Horses and Cattle, and Terrifying Inhabitants. St. Louis Globe Democrat.

About three weeks ago the *Globe Democrat* contained an account of a wonderful aquatic monster which was seen in the Mississippi River, near Quarantine Station, opposite the Government dike. The strange reptile was described by a number of persons who saw it as having a head similar to that of a dog and the bill of a pelican, through which it spouted a stream of water in the manner of a whale. It was observed to disport itself in the water for ten minutes, and then to disappear from view. The monster was reported to be all the way from thirty to one hundred feet in length. Of course, there were a large number of people ready to discredit this story, notwithstanding it was duly attested by many credible witnesses, prominent among whom was Mr. Eagan, one of the employees on the dike works, well known for his probity of character. Though a sharp lookout has been kept up by people living in the vicinity, no sign of the curious animal has been discovered since it disappeared, and even those who felt certain they had seen it began to suspect that they were victims of a too lively imagination. But a circumstance happened last Wednesday which no longer permits doubt that such a monster does inhabit the waters of the Mississippi, and that it is of even more fearful proportions than were first attributed to it. On that day a German farmer named Jacob Erst, living ten miles above St. Genevieve and fifty miles below St. Louis, was riding along the river bank, when he discovered an unusual and singular object stretched out on the sands, close by the water's edge. The river bank at this point is very low, starting at the edge of the water with a wide sand bar and extending at least 100 feet before reaching the low bluffs that serve as outer banks. Erst first took the object to be an immense cotton-wood log or tree that had been washed ashore by the last flood; but, seeing that it moved he soon discerned that it was an animate being of the most monstrous dimensions. Somewhat overcome by fear and excitement he galloped away in haste, and, reaching a neighbor's house, a few hundred yards distant, related his discovery. Upon a brief consultation it was decided that the neighbor and two grown sons and Mr. Erst should go back with guns, and see whether the monster was real or fancied. Arriving at the spot indicated, the reptile was discovered still stretched out on the sand, and not more than a hundred feet from where the men stood. It was the meridian of day, and the sun poured down its hottest rays.

The monster lay in the sand, sunning himself, and evidently oblivious to all surroundings. A hasty survey was taken by the party, and it was agreed that it was at least seventy feet in length. The head, as described by Eagan, was shaped much like that of a dog, but Mr. Erst maintains that it bore a still greater resemblance to that of a sea lion, though several times larger. The pelican shaped bill was also observable, and this was estimated to be five feet in length, being very sharp and pointed and having the appearance of an immense horn or tusk for use in offensive warfare. The body was the size of a flour barrel and covered with brown, shiny scales—as large as a human hand. Along the neck was also observed the mane, long and tangled like that of a horse. It had six legs, and on each side a huge fin or paddle. The tail was long, and gradually sloping to the end, which was set off with a spreading, fan-like fin, and the edges of the tail were indented so as to give it the semblance of a double-edged saw. Occasionally the monster shifted its position, as if to get more comfortably fixed, moving the feet carefully and one at a time, and swinging the tail around in a way that threw the dry sand in all directions. The horses that got a sight of it reared and plunged so they had to be taken to the rear and tied, the men returning to make further observations. For ten minutes the monster lay like a gigantic leviathan, with his short, angular legs outstretched and his immense tail whipping the sand like a mammoth broom. With this exception no portion of his body moved and he gave forth no sound save an occasional puff, loud and sonorous, similar to that of the sea-cow. The men watching it hallooed at different times, hoping to arrest its intention, but it did not again turn its eyes in that direction. A rifle shot, fired by one of the young men, James Stevens, had no more effect than if it had been a drop of water, the ball glancing off and falling far out into the river. Finally the men concluded to descend the bank and approach it from the rear. This they did with great caution, but had not proceeded more than thirty feet along the sand, when the monster for the first time, discovered that enemies were near and began moving. The outstretched legs were drawn up under the body, which swayed a moment or two like a floating log, and then, with a sudden motion, turned completely over, its new position being within five feet of the water. The men seeing that it was about to escape into the river, opened a broadside with three rifles and a shotgun. It was evident that the leviathan felt the volley, for he uttered a deep and tremulous snort as if in pain, and rolled over again, this time landing in shallow water. Immediately turning his head toward the current, he made rapid progress from the shore, puffing with a horrid noise and spouting water five or ten feet high, and shortly disappearing beneath the muddy waves. Where he swam the water seemed agitated as if by a whirlpool, and his enormous body sank so suddenly as to produce a suction like that accompanying the sinking of an over-freighted boat. About forty shots in all were fired, and when the men approached the spot where the monster had disported himself spots of blood were plainly visible in various places on the sand near the water's edge. This left no doubt that at least some of the shots had taken effect in vulnerable parts of the body, though it was exceedingly improbable that the monster had been vitally or seriously hurt. Along the shore, although the sand was beaten down hard and firm, a depression of at least four inches had been made where the stupendous body had laid. A measurement of the impression was taken by Mr. Stevens, and from where the forefeet rested to the point swept by the end of the tail it was sixty-one feet and three inches, leaving the head and body to be added, making an undoubted aggregate of seventy feet. An imprint of the foot showed that member to be webbed, and fourteen inches across, and possessed of claws several inches in length. In the wet sand, immediately at the water, the feet and legs had sunk at least twelve inches, leaving great quagmire holes nearly a foot and a half in diameter.

News of the phenomenal scene rapidly spread throughout the neighborhood, and at a late hour in the afternoon fully a hundred people had gathered at the spot, and parties were sent out one and two miles down the river to watch for another view of the monster.

Considerable excitement prevailed, and though there were two boats at hand, no one dared row out into the river. A report was prevalent that fifteen miles above, on the day before, a yawl boat, twenty feet in length, being rowed across the river by two men, was suddenly thrown into the air at least ten feet,

Southerners & Saurians

overturning the yawl and hurling both men into the river. The men swam to the boat, turned her over, bailed her out and got in, rowing as rapidly as possible to the shore. Another person present related how he had seen a horse, while swimming the river from the Illinois shore, suddenly disappear and rise no more, the subsequent inference being that he had been captured and swallowed by this colossal creature of the water. Another person stated that he had missed a valuable horse, which was in the habit of going to the river to drink, and still another narrated the singular fact that a neighbor of his had fished up from the shallow water, near the bark, the head and horns of a cow which had the appearance of being torn from the body. He had seen the same cow, an hour before, browsing on the bank.

In consequence of these discoveries, people living in that section are greatly excited, and there is very little crossing of the river for fear the aquatic monster may attack the boats and devour the occupants. A close watch is being kept along shore above and below St. Gene-vieve, and if human enterprise can accomplish the feat, the strange animal will not be captured or killed.

The next article came on October 5, 1877, via the *Chicago Daily Tribune* reprinting a report from the *St. Louis Globe-Democrat.*

St. Louis Globe-Democrat's River-Leviathan.

34

An Effort by the Mississippi to Get Ahead of Lake Michigan.
THAT MONSTER

Mr. Robert Mathison, a well-known business man of St. Louis, whose residence is at 2334 Olive street, arrived in the city last night by rail, from Memphis, and at a late hour called at the Globe-Democrat office and gave to a reporter a startling account of the recent exploits of the river monster which has created such an excitement during the last two weeks among the denizens of the Lower Mississippi. Mr. Mathison's narrative - and there seems to be no doubt of its literal truthfulness - is substantially as follows: Friday afternoon, at a late hour, - the sun being about a half-hour high, and the sky and air unusually clear, - Capt. John Carraway, of the towboat Bee Wing, having in tow six heavily-loaded coal-barges of the well-known Brown Barge & Transportation Company, of Pittsburgh, was passing a point on the river just above the village or landing known as Bradley's, five miles below Devil's Elbow Cut-off, and about fifteen miles above Memphis, when his attention was directed to a loud, puffing noise a considerable distance up the river. At first he thought it was the roaring of a broken 'scape-pipe or the wheezing of a disordered engine; but, seeing no smoke, and having reason to believe that there was no steam craft within hearing distance, below or above, he very shortly came to the conclusion that the sounds emanated from another source. Five minutes passed and the noise continued to be heard at brief intervals, and evidently getting closer. From the deck of the tow-boat a view could be had for 1,000 yards up the river, a gradual bend commencing at the distance. The sun was almost dipping below the western horizon when, around this bend, there rose to view the writing form of

A TERRIFIC MONSTER.

darting impetuously in mid-channel down the river. When first seen the leviathan seemed more like an immense uprooted tree, floating in a semi-perpendicular position along the mid-channel. As it neared, however, its horrid proportions became manifest. The hideousness of this aquatic monstrosity is stated by Capt. Carraway to be beyond the power of description. Its immense pelican bill, from five to ten feet in length, the gigantic bull-dog head, and the mammoth, slimy neck, upreared high in air; the vast tail lashing the water into fury, and the enormous fins, ten feet in length, sending out waves like the roll of a flying boat; the frequent dipping of the monstrous beak into the water, and spouting huge streams forty feet high in oblique directions, and the deep, cavernous roars that came thundering along at the briefest intervals - all these formed an infernal panorama that made the blood of the towboat Captain and his affrighted crew run cold, and their very hairs to stand on end. The

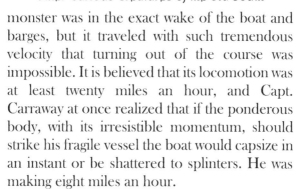

monster was in the exact wake of the boat and barges, but it traveled with such tremendous velocity that turning out of the course was impossible. It is believed that its locomotion was at least twenty miles an hour, and Capt. Carraway at once realized that if the ponderous body, with its irresistible momentum, should strike his fragile vessel the boat would capsize in an instant or be shattered to splinters. He was making eight miles an hour.

On the monster rushed, roaring with deafening effect, spouting from his horrid bill two streams of water that shot forty feet into the air, and fell in torrents into the river on either side.

THE SERPENTINE BODY

swayed tortuously and with frightful rapidity through the muddy waters, while the prodigious foreparts of the colossal reptile rose and sunk, and swayed like a Stygian horror, threatening to swallow and devour all that came within its reach. When within 150 or 200 yards, the horrid reptile, as if it had just discovered an obstacle in its track, slackened its precipitate pace, and for an instant paused to contemplate the nature of the obstruction. With a tremendous snort, so loud, and deep, and sonorous, that it gave the boat a tremulous motion, the huge creature came to a dead stop, and with its monstrous bill, head, and neck reared perpendicularly, seemed like a watery demon rising from the bosom of the deep. Here

Southerners & Saurians

Capt. Carraway, despite the terror that had necessarily taken possession of him, obtained a good view of the monster, at least the parts that were above the water, and his description of the horrible spectacle is sufficiently minute and accurate to deserve reproduction. Carraway alleges that there is no doubt the monster has a pelican-shaped bill, but that its length, which has heretofore been described as being five feet long, will measure at least ten feet. It appeared more like an immense horn than a beak, and in shape was much like the pointed sword of the spear-fish, though larger and longer, and decidedly more formidable as a weapon of offensive warfare. It was from through this bill that the monster spouted water, the water being thrown from a point near the head. Capt. Carraway, who is an old whaler, stated that

THE SPOUTING,

unlike that of the whale, which throws its stream upward in a straight column, was made in oblique directions, and that the volume of water spouted, and the height reached, was twice as great as that thrown by the whale. The head is described to have been four or five feet across, black and shining, and its shape bearing a close resemblance to that of the bulldog. Capt. Carraway thinks the animal bore on its head two short horns, but of this he is not certain, as the time for observation was very short. There could be no doubt, however, as to the canine shape of the head, and of the phenomenal circumstance that to this dog's head was attached a bill or beak, fashioned like that of a pelican. The neck appeared to be ten or twelve feet in length, narrow and serpentine, and swaying and writing with a motion like that of a snake poised in water. The sides and under portions of the neck were evidently covered with burnished scales of changeable hue, but from the top of the neck there grew what had the appearance of a mane, resembling that of a horse, being thick and shiny, and of a greenish tint. This mane reached from the base of the head to the body, and descended from the neck in long strands. These were the only parts of the body that were visible except the fins. On the back there appeared to be a dorsal fin, fifteen or twenty feet in length, measuring along the back, and perhaps three or four feet in height.

THE BODY,

being sunk in the water, however, could not be seen, and Capt. Carraway says he may be mistaken as to the dorsal fin, and only describes it as it appeared to him during the momentary opportunity he had for observation. The side fins were of monstrous proportions, extending fifteen feet on either side, and while the monster paused they rose and dipped back into the water rapidly, throwing immense waves in a forward direction, the monster by this means poising and steadying himself with the current.

This attitude was maintained not longer than three or four minutes, and the distance being nearly or quite 100 yards, Capt. Carraway's description is necessarily imperfect, but, in the main, it is undoubtedly accurate, as it agrees almost exactly with the description which has heretofore been given of the monster by persons who have seen him wading in shallow water or outstretched on sand-bars. Suddenly the immense head and neck disappeared under the water with a lashing sound that could have been heard a half-mile down the river. For a few moments nothing was seen of the monster, but it was quickly discovered that he was making, in a direct course, for the towboat and barges. His track was indicated by a rolling, pointed wave that came rushing forward like water impelled by a great submarine upheaval. There was great excitement on board, and the Captain and hands were all on deck, looking, with terror, upon the extraordinary spectacle. A young German, named Henry Decker, was on the coal barge lashed to the right of the towboat, and it was under this barge that the monster plowed his irresistible way. First came a violent shock and then the barge was thrown with tremendous force above the surface of the water and almost careened, the rear end being hoisted twenty feet into the air, half the cargo of coal being

HURLED INTO THE RIVER,

and along with it the man Henry Decker. The lashings by which the barge was secured to the towboat were snapped, and the shock was so sudden and strong that the towboat itself was almost lifted clear of the water. In a moment the monster reappeared in front of the fleet, and, turning its body so as to face the barge it had passed under, again reared its body, suddenly dived into the water, and made for the boats. It was a fortunate circumstance that the barge had become detached from the towboat; for this seems to be a special object of aversion to the leviathan, for he attacked it with a fury that was terrible to behold. First he dove into the sides with his huge beak, lifting it almost entirely out of the water, and sending it fifty feet away. Then he lashed it with his tail, the blows resounding with deafening effect, while in the meantime the air was made hideous with successive roars and harsh, loud bellows. A second time he made an assault with his beak, striking it fairly in the gunwales and sending it scudding 100 feet down the river. This last attack seemed to satisfy the monster, for, with a howl, he suddenly sunk beneath the surface and shot down the channel, going at a speed which Capt. Carraway affirms must have reached forty miles an hour. As he moved away no part of the body was visible, but the pointed wave that rolled before showed its course, while in its wake the waters rushed like those of a mill-dam

SUDDENLY LET LOOSE.

In two minutes he was out of sight. In the meantime, Henry Decker, the hand who was precipitated from the barge, swam to another barge and clambered safely up the sides, with no greater damage than a thorough drenching and a slight contusion on the head, made by a falling piece of coal. The engine had been stopped when the first shock came. It was put in motion as soon as it was apparent that the danger had passed, and Capt. Carraway set about securing the detached barge. By the time he reached it it was 300 yards down the river, and in a sinking condition. The front end had already sunk, and the stern was raised ten feet above the water. As the towboat approached the wreck swung around, and a close view showed that the bottom had been ripped in a half-dozen places, the portions of the gunwales still out of the water were split and splintered as if an ax had been used to cut and tear them to pieces. At one point the gunwale was torn off the entire depth. As the towboat floated against the wreck, one of the hands called Capt. Carraway's attention to a strange object that protruded from the rear end of the boat. It had the appearance of a huge splinter, but its appearance was so singular that Capt. Carraway's curiosity was aroused, and he steamed immediately by the object, in order to see what it was. Upon a close view, it was discovered that it was nothing more nor less than a piece of the monster's bill, which had been splintered off and left in the gunwale of the boat. An effort was made to pull the splinter out, but this undertaking was found too difficult to accomplish, as it was driven entirely through the timber, and was as fast and hard as if it were part and parcel of the barge. Axes were brought, and the gunwale chopped down on either side, and the piece containing the splinter split off. An examination showed the splinter to be four feet long, and undoubtedly a piece of

THE MONSTER'S BILL.

At one end it was twelve inches broad, gradually sloping until it reached a sharp point. It was quite thin and looked as if it might be a mere outward covering for the end of the lower part of the bill. It was neither horn nor bone, but appeared more like ivory, though almost as tough and hard as steel. In color it was dark green and brown, mixed and varied though the larger end was almost black. The piece weighed eighteen pounds, this heavy weight showing the unusual compactness of the material composing the beak.

An hour was spent at the wreck, when Capt. Carraway, seeing that the coal was a total loss and the barge in such a condition that he could do nothing then to save it, steamed on, reaching Memphis about 9 o'clock at night, where he related his strange adventure and exhibited the splinter from the monster's bill. Of course, the majority of people are skeptical about stories relating to monsters, and many were incredulous, but those who knew Capt. Carraway felt certain that whatever he might relate could be depended on as truthful in every respect.

There certainly cannot be longer doubt that the Mississippi is inhabited with a monster that

not only ranks in horrid proportions with the fabled creatures of fiction, but one that may do much to interfere with free and uninterrupted commerce on the great river. It is undeniable that among river men there is a feeling of insecurity, and it has been suggested that the matter is of such importance that an expedition ought to be organized under Government management to hunt down and annihilate the leviathan. The New Madrid Gazette (from which place the Globe- Democrat published a special dispatch concerning exploits of the monster) of Wednesday says that a number of valuable horses and cattle were

MYSTERIOUSLY DESTROYED

while the monster haunted that part of the river, that no less than three boats were overturned, and one skiff shattered and its occupant drowned.

The Vicksburg Pilot publishes an interview with Capt. Cuthbert, of the Ohio River trade, in which the Captain states that at a point ten miles above Henderson the monster attacked a flatboat, overturning the boat and throwing the ferryman and two passengers and their horses into the river. One of the men was drowned and the monster devoured one of the horses. These stories seem almost incredible, but they are so fortified by the testimony of unimpeachable witnesses, that all unbelief is necessarily dissipated.

THE MONSTER HEARD FROM AGAIN.

MEMPHIS, Tenn., Sept. 20. - A report was current yesterday morning that the river monster, which attacked Capt. Carraway's barges, had been seen to pass the Memphis wharf, though as the rumor could not be traced to a positive and reliable source, it was generally discredited. A courier just in from Flournoy's Landing, fifteen miles below here, and three miles below President's Island, brings intelligence that it was seen to pass that point at 4 o'clock this afternoon, and that it was traveling at a furious rate down the river, with its head high in the air, and bellowing so loud that it was plainly heard a mile away. No more damage has been done by it, so far as could be learned.

FISHERMAN AND RAFT ON MISSISSIPPI RIVER NEAR ST. LOUIS, MISSOURI C.1930S. LIBRARY OF CONGRESS.

Southerners & Saurians

Next that we hear of the creature comes from the January 12, 1878 *Montana Helena Independent.*

THE RIVER MONSTER.
It Attacks a Produce Boat on the Mississippi River.
A Good View of the Huge Saurian.
From the Nachez Democrat

A few weeks ago we published the particulars of a sea monster, as related by a towboat captain. The captain of a towboat described the monster as resembling an immense snake with a bulldog head and a pelican bill about ten feet long. It lashed the water into foam with its tail, and spouted oblique streams of water forty feet high. The monster attacked the barge which the towboat had in tow. After it disappeared the captain examined the barge, and found a splinter from its bill embedded in the timber, winch he said resembled ivory.

At the time of publishing the above we felt a little inclined to doubt the monster story, but now, after having ourselves interviewed two gentlemen who have seen it, we really think there is a big sea monster in the Mississippi river.

The gentlemen whom we interviewed say that on the night of the 9th inst., while floating down the Mississippi river on Capt. Ed Baker's produce boat, when near Island No. 25, they

46

were startled by a very loud splash in the water, and as they had heard of the great monster, they were very much frightened. They saw a dark object not more than eighty yards from the boat, and for the first time saw the huge monster. It was swimming at a pretty fast rate towards the boat, and it made as much noise as the steamer R.E. Lee. It came on, and as it neared the boat it suddenly veered to the right, striking the stern oar and knocking it overboard. John Laughlin and Dud. Kelley alone remained on the boat, the balance of the crew taking refuge in the cabin. The monster came near enough to enable those two gentlemen to get a full view of him. They judged him to be sixty-five feet in length. Its body was shaped like a snake, its tail forked like a fish, and had a bill like that of a pelican. Its bill was fully six feet in length, he had a long, flowing black mane like a horse. When he swam his head was eight feet above the water. It was a grand sight to see him move down the river. Messrs. Callahan and Kelly tells us that it was impossible to induce the crew to come out that night. The pilot, Mr. McCune George, was finally led out by his wife, she assuring him that the great monster had departed.

Capt. Baker's boat is now moored at our landing at the foot of Main Street. All of his crew except one man has abandoned her, and Captain Baker says it is impossible to find a crew as the men think the monster is still following them.

NOTE THAT THIS CREATURE SIGHTED
IN AN ARKANSAS CAVE HAD FOUR LEGS
AND TWO FLIPPERS LIKE THE
MISSISSIPPI MONSTER.

Swamp Monsters, Lizard Men, and
Other Curious Creatures of the Old South

Overall the article is encouraging because the descriptions and measurements all line up with the previous articles. With this in mind, we can ascertain one of two things. Either witnesses all saw the same, real monster. Or, the same writer made up all three stories and kept his details consistent.

Let's overview the basics of the creature once again from article to article. In the first account, the creature was estimated to be 30 feet long, and had a head like a dog's but with the beak of a pelican measuring one foot long. The ears were noted as distinct, and being like those of a dog or a sea lion. It was described as having scales that were either black or dark brown, with a bottom portion that was dark blue like a catfish. The creature appeared to have four legs and two larger flippers, making for six appendages in all.

The second article acknowledged the comparisons to a dog's head, but the witnesses argued that it looked more like a seal's head, which makes more sense. The bill, estimated to be one foot long in the first encounter, was bumped up to five feet. Again, brown scales were observed, as were six appendages. This time the tail could be seen which terminated in a fluke, similar to a whale's.

The third article struck me as odd. The first two gave me no indication of a plesiosaur-like creature with the traditional long neck. This report did, as it claimed the monster was swimming "semi perpendicular" out of the water. Furthermore, the pelican bill had grown again to ten feet. The captain who recorded the sighting also added in a new feature not yet discussed as he observed two short horns on the head, a common attribute of Nessie and other lake monsters, by the way.

ZEUGLODONS IN WATER.

What we have is a true anomaly. There is no dinosaur that looks like what was described. If anything, it sounds like an amalgam of a plesiosaurs and a zeuglodon. If it weren't for the plesiosaur-like neck, a zeuglodon would almost be a fitting candidate. Though snake-like, zeuglodons did not have a long neck (though some early reconstructions depicted them as though they did).

Perhaps the most maddening thing about the Mississippi monster is that it exhibits traits distinct to both reptiles and whales. The scales and snake-like neck could only belong to a reptile, but the fluke tail and ability to spout water is a cetacean trait. But, dinosaurs aren't our only option. There are plenty of sea serpents that don't fit the descriptions plesiosaurs, zeuglodons, kronosaurs, etc. Some would seem to be completely unknown animals.

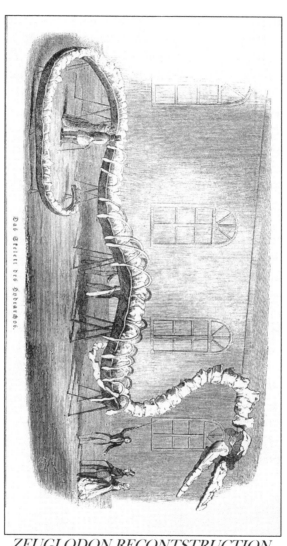

ZEUGLODON RECONTSTRUCTION.

Southerners & Saurians

The Sea Centipede (which is a reptile, not a bug) is a good example, and like the Mississippi Monster had more than four appendages. Patrick Huyghe and Loren Coleman discussed the creature in their book, *Field Guide to Lake Monsters, Sea Serpents and Other Mystery Denizens of the Deep.*

The creature is described as 30 to 60 feet in length with "lateral projections, plates, or fins that stick out prominently from its sides."[3] The Sea Centipede was also said to shoot water vapor from its nose or mouth area, and this Mississippi beastie does the same.

Sea Centipedes aside, if the monster has any cousins out there, the closest that I can find is the famous Moore's Beach monster that washed ashore dead in 1925. The monster washed up on Natural Bridges State Beach in Monterey Bay, California, where it was found by Charles Moore.

Its descriptions vaguely match the Mississippi Monster, mainly being the head which had small eyes and a duck-like beak (though not as pointed as the Mississippi Monster's). The neck portion was about 20-30 feet long. The carcass had blunt, elephant-like legs, though other witnesses claimed they were more like flippers. Like the Mississippi Monster, it had a tail fluke similar to a whale.

---

[3] Coleman and Huyghe, *Lake Monsters and Sea Serpents*, pp.152.

MOORE'S BEACH MONSTER C.1925.

A renowned naturalist of the time, E. L. Wallace, studied the creature and declared that it wasn't a whale but might be some type of plesiosaur— possibly preserved in a glacier somewhere. The skull of the monster was given to the California Academy of Sciences, which claimed that it was really a rare type of large beaked whale, *Berardius bairdi*. And perhaps it was, as the carcass does indeed look like that same species of beaked whale.

This still doesn't answer our question as to what the Mississippi monster was, though. The animal,

as far as I can tell, disappeared from headlines in the *St. Louis Globe-Democrat* after 1878. But, there's still more to the story. A creature matching the Mississippi River monster's description was spotted in the Ohio River at the exact same time.

The witness, Ben Karrick, wrote to the *Cincinnati Gazette* and described a monster with a head and neck "covered by a black glossy substance like hair..." He described the hide as looking like that of an alligator's. However, rather than a bulldog, he compared the head to that of a sea horse.

As a believer, one could argue that this lends credibility to the monster, as this was possibly a

Southerners & Saurians

member of the same species.[4] If one wants to take a skeptical approach, just as easily the argument could be made that it was just a copycat article using a very similar monster design.

However, Karrick wasn't the only one who saw the monster. The same day that Karrick saw it, so did John Davidson, captain of the *Silver Moon* steamboat. Davidson wrote to the *Cincinnati Enquirer* (remember, Karrick wrote to the *Gazette*) and told them:

> "At one time [the monster] reared its head high above the surface of the water in the manner of the sea lions of the Zoological Gardens of your city. The long pelican beak, the slimy mane, and the extreme serpentine length of the animal answer exactly to the previous descriptions that have been published."

The long beak? The slimy mane? This is a dead ringer for the Mississippi Monster. Either it switched rivers, or a newspaper writer in Cincinnati decided to perpetrate a river monster hoax with the Mississippi creature as their template.

As usual, we will never know.

Sources:

Coleman, Loren and Patrick Huyghe. *The Field Guide to Lake Monsters, Sea Serpents, and Other Mystery Denizens of the Deep.* New York: Tarcher/Penguin, 2003.

---

[4] As the monster was sighted in the Mississippi around this same time, it would have to be a different creature.

SOUTHERN SNAIK STORIES
Capturing a Sea Serpent

The following story came from the *Cedar Rapids Evening Gazette* on August 21, 1896, on page three:

Captured a Sea Serpent
Town Steamer Fifteen Miles in Gulf Water
Before It Is Killed

Carrabelle, Fla., Aug. 21—On the wharf in this town is a great sea serpent, which was killed in the gulf yesterday after it had towed the steamer Crescent City for over an hour at a terrific pace. The monster is a horrible looking object. It measures forty-nine feet and two inches in length, and is seventy-two inches around its body in the largest part. It is eel-shaped, with the exception of its head and tail. It has a spoon-bill-shaped head, with a mouth resembling a shark's, except that it is a great deal larger. Its teeth are set at an angle of about forty-five degrees backwards in the mouth, and it has a long forked tongue. The tail is armed with formidable fins six to eight inches long. The color is brown, with a greenish back, making it appear black in the water. The underside is yellow.

The Crescent City left here yesterday morning for the snapper banks off Dog island, with about 100 excursionists on board. Shortly after the boat left a line, to which was attached a shark hook baited with mullet was thrown overboard near the bow. The hook was almost immediately seized by some thing which darted ahead at a tremendous gait. The line attached to the hook was nearly 600 yards long, but it became tangled after 100 yards had been paid out and the boat was then at the mercy of the monster, which made seaward, pulling the steamer, which is only a six-knot boat, at fully twelve knots an hour. The passengers became panic-stricken and urged the captain to cut the line, but he refused saying he was resolved to capture the monster.

Three times the monster sank down and it looked as if the Crescent City would be submerged. So deep was it pulled into the water that great waves rolled over the decks. When the monster was within twenty yards of the Crescent City passengers and crew poured shot after shot, and finally killed it. It was then hauled on board and the steamer brought it here.

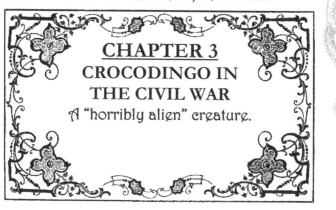

CHAPTER 3
CROCODINGO IN
THE CIVIL WAR
A "horribly alien" creature.

Quite simply, I don't know what to make of this story nor the creature described therein. It is called the Crocodingo, and is essentially a dingo with the head of a crocodile. If you think that's weird, just wait until you hear its origin story.

On the night of July 31, 1839, a farmer named Hank Lemon had what could be considered an alien encounter in Huntsville, Tennessee. Lemon noticed a strange green glow in the sky behind his home, which was comparable to the Northern Lights. Ominously, his dogs seemed disturbed by the strange light. And then, "a dead straight bolt of lightning" hit the ground. The green glow dissipated, and moments later he saw a strange "horribly alien" looking creature dart from the woods. He described it as having the body of a dog with the head of a crocodile.

Lemon also reported on a horrible stench, stating, "There was this horrible charnel stench in the air, and something else...a horrible thing....something that would drive a man crazy should he be exposed to it for too long a period."

The creature was spotted sporadically from 1856 to 1860 in the vicinity of New River, Tennessee. Curiously, the creature was observed catching fish from a creek quite often. Some fishermen even left fish out for the animal as an offering of a sort. Initially, the creature was known as the Haint Dog. In the late 1800s, Curiel Allan Brown, whose father was an Australian immigrant, nicknamed the strange animal the "Crocodingo."

A notable encounter with a Crocodingo occurred during the Civil War. A Confederate soldier named Roger Owens stated that he observed the Crocodingo guarding a freshly mauled soldier (presumably, the corpse was the creature's kill). When Owens returned later, he found only blood. The body and the dog were gone.

Other Confederate soldiers reported seeing the beast, claiming that it watched them from afar and sometimes growled at them. Or, if not that, they might catch a glimpse of it running through the woods.

The sightings continued after the war, too. In the early 1900s, the dwindling fish population near New River was attributed to the monster. Farmers shot at the animal and set traps for it, but nothing ever came of these endeavors.

CROCODINGO.

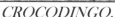

As time carried on, so did the Crocodingo. Railroad workers in the vicinity of Oneida, Tennessee, claimed to find newly laid rails with bite marks in them, which they attributed to the Crocodingo. Sometimes the rails were split in two.

Sightings reached a peak in 1925, after the implementation of the Oneida Sewer System. Locals began to report strange cries coming from the sewer drains. These horrible "alien cries" would come about after a heavy rain. The next day, manholes would be found overturned, implying something crawled its way out of the sewers.

A man named Jack Bannister claimed that he followed a strange animal that he at first mistook for a coyote into the sewer in 1943. He said that it had dog-like mannerisms and nudged open the manhole and then "slithered down into the sewer." And yes, Bannister did say that he got a clear look at the animal, which had the body of a "mangy wolf" but with the head of an alligator or crocodile. The next significant sighting would not occur until the next century, in 2012, when two witnesses saw the animal emerge from a utility hole.

Solely because of the Hank Lemon account, many people associate the Crocodingo with extraterrestrials. The theory is that the animal is a genetic hybrid cross between a crocodile and a dog created by aliens!

However, if we discard the green glow in the sky as a coincidence, and examine this creature as though it were a prehistoric survivor, a likely candidate could be a member of the therapsid family of reptiles, specifically the Cynognathus. As the book *Dinosaurs and Other Prehistoric Animals* so succinctly puts it, the animal "looked like a cross between a wolf and a lizard."[5] Artists have rendered the animals in various ways over the years, but it is essentially a hairy quadruped dinosaur that has the stance of a dog, but the elongated head and mouth of a carnivorous reptile, like a crocodile. As people in the nineteenth century were no doubt unfamiliar with such an animal, they might well have described it simply as a dog with the head of the biggest, fiercest reptile that they knew: the crocodile.

[5] Mehling, *Dinosaurs*, pp.72.

THERAPSIDS BY CHARLES KNIGHT.

Other theories tie the beast in with the Bell Witch Legend, also out of Tennessee. As to why this is, the Bell Witch legend began with a cryptid sighting. A man named John Bell spotted a dog with the head of a rabbit outside his home in 1817. Soon after this, the house was plagued by the ghost of a woman named Kate. In addition to the loquacious spirit, there were other supernatural occurrences, such as an invisible animal gnawing on bedposts and the sounds dogs fighting outside where there weren't any. However, the association with the Bell Witch legend is a tenuous one, probably simply because they occurred in the same state and involve a dog-like cryptid. In this same supernatural vein, others theorize the Crocodingo is a type of Native American skinwalker.[6]

---

[6] On that note, the Bell Witch at one point claimed she was awakened due to a disturbance at an Indian burial ground on Bell's property. The Crocodingo, for some reason, is associated with a spot called "The Witch's Grave."

Southerners & Saurians

The biggest problem with the Crocodingo isn't its identity or origin. It's the lack of sources. Though online articles on the beast are many, absolutely none of the articles cite sources! I can find no newspaper articles reporting on any of the sightings.[7] As such, I would imagine that the Crocodingo is simple folklore and nothing more.

Sources:

Mehling, Carl (Ed.). *Dinosaurs and Other Prehistoric Animals.* Amber Books, 2018.

Swancer, Brent. "Curious Mystery Monsters of the American Civil War." Mysterious Universe. (February 3, 2016) https://mysteriousuniverse.org/2016/02/curious-mystery-monsters-of-the-american-civil-war/

---

[7] It's possible the Crocodingo story was first unearthed by Edgar Riley in his book *The Civil War of the Worlds: First-Hand Accounts of UFOs and Other Mysterious Phenomena During America's Civil War.* This book, like the Crocodingo, is nowhere to be found so far, a rarity in the age of Amazon and EBay.

CHAPTER 4
BAYOU
BEAST
"A Roarer of the Reeds."

L ake Catherine is a brackish-water lake[8] located within the vicinity of the current day New Orleans, Louisiana, city limits. But, back in 1883, it was still wild territory. So wild, in fact, that it harbored a monster. The *Burlington Hawk Eye* reported the following on June 27, 1883, on page six:

A Roarer of the Reeds.
New Orleans Times-Democrat.

Last Saturday G. B. Shaw, of Vermilion parish, and Will Cook, Frank Hansen and Fritz, the keeper of the Lake Catherine club, were out

---

[8] Brackish-water meaning that it has more salinity than freshwater, but not as much as seawater.

hunting on Bayou Bobb, Lake Catherine, when their attention was attracted by a great disturbance in the waters of the bayou. Rushing to the bank of the stream they saw, beyond the reeds, which grew out into the water, a reptile, whose immensity and revolting ugliness amazed them beyond measure. As nearly as could be judged from that portion of the monster which was exposed above the water it was thirty feet long: its breadth in the thickest part about three feet; its back was rough and corrugated with mottled and horny barbs, apparently from six to ten inches long, studded thickly down what was evidently the column of a vertebrate. The tail was not visible, but its length was made apparent by the movement of the waters as the monster used it in propelling itself rapidly down the bayou. The proboscis and eyes were visible and in shape and position seemed much like those of an alligator. As the monster moved great waves were raised and broke among the reeds.

Their guns were heavily loaded, fortunately, with buckshot. At the first fire there was a terrific result. The waters of the broad bayou were lathed from bank to bank and the great waves shook the reeds as a strong wind. The monster reared its huge, repulsive head a full six feet above the water, and its red, glittering eyes glared fiercely toward its enemies. They were almost paralyzed with the horror of the dreadful apparition, but directly summoned the nerve to fire their second barrel at the frightful muzzle of the monster, which, wide open displayed a cavernous throat, from which flashed a long slender tongue. As the smoke cleared from this second discharge it was seen that the monster had again subsided and its huge back passed through the water with incredible swiftness toward an unusually thick and broad knap of reeds, some score of yards down the stream and on the opposite side. As it disappeared the gentlemen were still further terrified with a muffled roar. They hastened to the spot opposite that at which the monster had disappeared and confirmed to fire into the reeds for a long while in the hope that the monster would reappear, but it was of no avail and none of the party thinking the occasion demanded a nearer approach, they departed.

G.B. SHAW.

Though I can't say with certainty that the monster was real, G.B. Shaw was. He served as the seventh

Sheriff of the Vermilion Parish from 1868 to 1872. After that, he also served as a tax collector and was also a nationally ranked marksman (perhaps those two things went hand in hand?).

The fact that Shaw was known for being a marksman is illuminating for me. So let's say that a newspaper writer made up a story starring Shaw facing off against a monster—or possibly that Shaw himself made it up in good fun—you've got an expert marksman, why not use that in the story? Had this story been made up, I have a feeling it would have utilized this better. For instance, maybe Shaw would have shot the creature between the eyes. Then the article could have ended with the perennial promise to ship off the monster to the Smithsonian as so many of them did. But it didn't. In fact, it's not really that exciting of an encounter as far as these old articles go. Witnesses see monster, witnesses shoot at monster, monster leaves—end of story. In my opinion, were this story made up it would've been more fantastical.

A LESS THORNY RENDITION OF A DESMATOSUCHUS.

The monster's credibility isn't too shabby either. Unlike the mystery creatures covered in the past three chapters, the creature described here matches almost perfectly with a known dinosaur. Though I'm sure a spiky backed ankylosaur came to mind initially when reading about the animal, the head was described as crocodilian by the witnesses. An ankylosaur's head is most certainly not comparable to a crocodile's. Enter the lesser know Desmatosuchus, which essentially looks like a Crocodile with spikes along its back. In fact, the name even translates to mean "link crocodile." Despite its intimidating appearance, it was an herbivore, and the spikes were likely to protect it from carnivores.

The dimensions of the creature don't match up perfectly with a Desmatosuchus, which was supposed to max out at a little under twenty feet in length. But, the witnesses only estimated the creature to be 30 feet long, they never confirmed it because part of its body was under the water. The length of the spines on the back they estimated to be six to ten inches long, and the Desmatosuchus had spikes that were 18 inches in length. Bigger, certainly, but close enough to the other measurements. The only thing against the Desmatosuchus being the candidate for the creature is that the beast had two huge shoulder spikes that surely the witnesses would have commented on.

Desmatosuchus or not, I think this was a legitimate sighting of something.

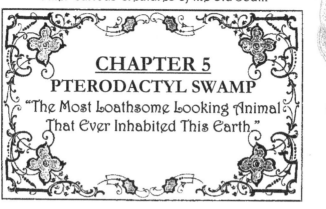

CHAPTER 5
PTERODACTYL SWAMP
"The Most Loathsome Looking Animal That Ever Inhabited This Earth."

I n the realm of remnant dinosaur sightings, the two most common varieties that are sighted are the plesiosaurus and various members of the pterosaur family. For that reason, whenever I come across an old newspaper article that deals with either of those creatures it tends to boost the story's credibility in my eyes, as opposed to something more obscure like an Iguanodon in Death Valley.

That said, something seems fishy about this pterosaur story reported in the *Atlanta Constitution* on February 11, 1895.

A Strange Animal

"It was about 8 o'clock in the morning, and I was standing with my gun behind some trees, about a hundred yards from the outside, waiting to get a shot if possible at a passing deer. Suddenly I heard a noise in towards the river that made my hair stand on end. It was not such a loud noise, nor did it sound very dangerous— but it was peculiar; I had never heard anything like it before, and I hope I may never hear it again. It was a sound somewhat like the quacking of a duck and the hissing of a snake combined. That is as near as I can describe it, and yet that does not give any idea of how it sounded. It was stronger and louder than either, and yet that is the impression that it gave me— either that it must be a monster duck or a huge snake; and then I thought it must be both.

"The sound seemed to issue from a thick place surrounding a kind of lagoon. I kept my eyes fastened on the spot with cocked gun in hand. I had not long to wait. In a few seconds I heard a kind of splashing in the water and peering through the bushes I saw, about a hundred yards away, what seemed to be the head of an enormous duck. But I thought surely it was the king of all ducks—for the bill was at least a foot long and as black as could be. It was still making that blood-curdling, half-hissing, half-quacking noise, and seemed to be wading or swimming slowly along in the mud and water.

"Before I had time to think—even if my brain had been in any condition for such work—the creature raised itself up a little and I saw the blackest, ugliest, most loathsome-looking animal that ever inhabited this earth, I do firmly believe. Its body was between three and four feet long and was also black. When I first caught a glimpse of it I thought I must have been mistaken in the head and that it was an alligator coming out to sun himself; and yet I had never seen an alligator like that before.

"Coming on up nearer to where I crouched in terror behind a tree I soon had an opportunity to see the thing in all its strangeness and ugliness. There was a little knoll where the puddle of water ended, and—horror of borrows [sic]—what I had thought was an alligator stepped up on this little elevation, and I then saw that it had only two feet. As near as I could judge, its legs were about a foot and a half long, and it stood there like some huge blackbird in the night, with its bill stuck downward and still emitting that unearthly kind of noise.

"To say that I was paralyzed with fear would hardly give you an idea of my condition. If the creature had seen me and started in my direction, I am sure I would never have been alive when it reached me. It never occurred to me that my gun would have been any protection; I was so completely terrified by the appearance of the unnatural looking thing that I couldn't think of anything else. I believe I would rather have braved a thousand alligators than that bird, or beast, or whatever you might call it.

"It stood there, I suppose, about a minute, and I had a good opportunity to examine it with my eye. Its body was tough and scaly, like an alligator's, and the tail went off to a point. It had legs like a turkey or duck, only they were larger and stronger; its feet I could not see on account of some bushes. It kept turning its bill up and down and around, but try as I could I never did locate its eyes. They were the features I was right then most interested in not seeing, and I suppose they were so black that at that distance I could not make them out.

"I can never describe the awful sound the thing made with its mouth. It made my blood run colder every time I heard it. After a short while, that seemed an age, the creature gave a kind of spring from the ground, and before I could realize what it was doing it went up into a large tree and sat on the lowest limb. As it did so, I could hardly believe my eyes when I saw two dark wings spread out from its side and strike the air with a heavy sound that made my heart sick. I had not noticed before that it had wings, but wings they certainly were, although I could see no feathers. As soon as it had poised itself on the limb its wings were drawn so closely to its body that it was impossible to detect where they were. I looked at it for a second or two, and then as its back was towards me, I thought it was a favorable opportunity to get out of the swamp, as I was hungry anyhow. I stuck quietly out and never took a long breath until I had left the swamp a full half mile behind."

Though this seems like a routine enough sighting, I have some issues with it. For starters, the "witness" is a suspiciously good writer. So good, I think the witness was really just a newspaper writer cooking up a good yarn. To his credit, the beast wasn't magnified to proportions so great that it knocked it out of the realm of credibility. This was the case of the 1890 Tombstone Thunderbird story, in which the alleged pterosaur measured over 90 feet long when the biggest member of the pterodactyl family could only reach 30 feet. So, the size of the animal was about right for a Pterodactylus, which often had three-foot wingspans. That the witness described the creature as scaly hurts the credibility, though. Most pterodactyls are thought to have sported coats of hair-like filaments known as pycnofibers, not scales.

This story also came on the heels of two other well-publicized pterosaur stories. The 1890 Tombstone story I already mentioned, but there was another from Fresno, California, in 1891. In that case, the pterosaurs were also sighted in a swampy area.

But, I should reiterate that these are my own skeptical assumptions of the case. Like Mulder on *The X-Files*, I want to believe but have learned to be cautious of these stories overall. For all the reasons I stated above, my instincts tell me this is a work of fiction.

SOUTHERN SNAIK STORIES
Mysterious Merman

The following story came from the *Shelbyville Daily Evening Democrat* on September 29, 1882, on page three, and tells of what sounds to be a real-life Gillman.

A Strange Animal in Florida

A strange animal, half man and half fish, and covered with a long growth of coarse black hair, has been seen several times recently in Big Charley Popka river, Manitee county, Florida. The head and upper portion of the body resemble a man, short, stumpy arms, with webbed feet taking the place of fins, while the lower portion is just like the tail of any fish. The monstrosity is about four feet in length, and when sporting about in the water utters coarse, guttural sounds, a cross between the barking of a dog and the bellowing of a bull. Several attempts to capture and shoot the animal have proven futile.

CHAPTER 6
SAILING SERPENTS OF THE SOUTH
"Scared Out of Their Wits by an Alleged Flying Serpent."

lying snakes are one of the harder cryptids to pin down for researchers because, frankly, they just don't make sense. Some of them have wings—which explains the flying—but many more do not as some witnesses claim to see literal snakes slithering through the air somehow! Some are gigantic, while others are of a normal size. And how do they fly? Nobody knows. But the articles are out there, and they are many. Here are a selected few from the Southern States (which have been edited to remove unfortunate racial slurs).

First, from the May 31, 1888 *Dunkirk Observer Journal:*

South Carolina [Residents] Scared Out of Their Wits by an Alleged Flying Serpent

Southerners & Saurians

COLUMBIA, May 31.—There comes a story from Darlington County, this State, of a flying serpent.

Monday evening just before sunset Miss Ida Davis and her two younger sisters were strolling through the woods when they were suddenly startled by the appearance of a huge serpent moving through the air above them. The uncanny creature was distant only two or three rods when they first beheld, and was sailing through the air with a speed equal to that of a hawk or a buzzard, but without any visible means of propulsion. Its movements and its flight resembled those of the snake, and looked a formidable object as it wound its way along, being apparently about 15 feet in length and as large around as a good-sized human thigh.

The girls stood amazed and followed it with their eyes until it was lost to view in the distance. The flying serpent was also seen by a number of people in another part of the country early in the afternoon of the same day, and by these it is represented as admitting a hissing noise, which could be distinctly heard. The [African American population] in that section are greatly excited over the matter. Religious revival meetings have been inaugurated in their churches, and many of them declare that the day of judgment is near at hand.

Years later, the *Branford Opinion* ran the following on Saturday, August 7, 1897:

A Flying Snake is Reported from South Carolina.

The Hartsville correspondent of The News and Courier describes it in detail as follows:

"The flying snake was seen near Newman swamp by a Mr. Odom on Sunday afternoon, at 6 o'clock. This is about ten miles south of this place. Later, say 7 o'clock on the same day, it was seen by Mr. Henry Polson, in Chesterfield county, twelve miles north of here. Mr. Polson says: 'The monster was low down, just above the tree tops; had its head thrown back in position to strike, and was just floating through the atmosphere lengthwise.' He says it seemed to be twenty-five to forty feet long and about eight to ten inches through at the largest part. In the language of Mr. Polson, 'he do not say it was a snake, but he do say it was the most like a snake of anything he ever saw, and he believes it was a snake.' There are all kinds of opinions as to what the monster could be. Everyone in lower Chesterfield almost is giving out an opinion, but the most original explanation is from my friend, William J. Johnson, a near neighbor of Mr. Polson. He says it was surely the devil going on to Washington to look after Ben Tillman and the Tariff bill. Mr. Johnson says the snake was seen near Chesterfield courthouse and also in several towns in North Carolina. "

Southerners & Saurians

And here is yet another story, this time about a winged snake, from the *Daily Iowa State Press* published on June 15, 1899, on page two:

Snake 35 feet long, with wings.

Policeman O'Brien of New York has received a letter from a friend in Everglades, Fla., describing a monster seen there recently. O'Brien's correspondent calls the thing a "flying snake." He says it was first seen by the McCorkle brothers, whom O'Brien knows well, as they were walking through their orange grove. "The snake rose from the top of an old orange tree," says the writer, "and started circling westward. It was about 35 feet long and had four wings, a skull like a puff adder, a bald pate, tapering tail, eyes that flashed fire, a tongue that was plainly venomous, and a look of dark – blue annoyance." O'Brien's correspondent adds that the sober citizens of the place had formed a hunt club and are making plans to bag the snake.

I would quickly dismiss flying snakes as the products of newspaper writers, but many cultures from around the world tell of flying snakes, the highest concentration being in the Middle East. So, there could be more truth to these Southern Serpent sightings than we know.

SOUTHERN SNAIK STORIES

Monster of Goose Lake

The following story came from the *Chester Daily Times* on October 25, 1881:

A Monster Unlike Anything
Ever Seen or Heard of Before

Fishing parties at Goose Lake, Florida, tell of a monster unlike anything ever seen or heard of before. J. Z. Scott first saw it, and says that it has a body between fifteen and twenty feet in length, and as large around as a common horse. It has a head like a dog and tail like a catfish. No fins or feet have ever been observed, though it seems to move with the motion of a fish, rather than that of a snake. All those portions of the body which have been exposed are covered with long hair of a dark color. It swims with astonishing rapidity, and will follow a lighted boat at night. Messrs. Aaron Terry and N. G. Osborne were out in a boat gig fishing, when the monster approached within striking distance, and they drove the gig deeply into it. The animal freed itself with a violent effort, twisting the prongs of the gig like so many straws.

CHAPTER 7
WRIGHT RIVER
DINOSAUR
"A creature almost
indescribable."

Though perhaps not as exciting as the last few chapters, the story presented here might just be more credible. Because the sad fact of the matter is, the more exciting the story is, the less likely it is to be true. The men in this story didn't claim to be attacked by the fantastic animal they saw, nor did they themselves attack it and vow to send the body to the Smithsonian, etc., etc. The following story is simple, and I also believe it to be true.

The creature described sounds every bit like a plesiosaur-type creature except for the feet, which are just that and not flippers, meaning it could have been an Apatosaurus of some sort. The story was printed in the *Morning Oregonian* on May 13, 1870.

A Hideous Sea Monster

A PARTY COMING TO [Savannah, Georgia] from South Carolina through Wright river in a small sail boat manned by three oarsmen, has furnished us with a decidedly sensational account of his adventures with one of the most [indecipherable] of creatures that ever crawled or floated under the firmament of heaven, and assures us positively that he has not been deceived by any freak of fancy or undue excitement of mind.

"Our informant, on the morning of the 28th [of February], toward noon, as he tells us, was about half a mile from Wright river, a stream merging into the Savannah, two miles above Fort Pulaski, with his oarsmen pulling quietly along near the shore, when the slight built craft was suddenly and without any premonitory sign lifted up, as if by some immense roller, throwing the crew out of their seats and completely scaring the life out of them. The shock was so sudden that danger existed for a second of the boat turning over, but luckily it righted again and sank back into the water, which foamed like breakers.

"'But,' says the hero of the adventure, 'I did not heed the danger around me in this respect, nor the groveling fear of the men with me, for I could not, if my life was at stake, have taken my eyes away from the hideous creature that had caused all the commotion, and was making its way lazily out of the river into the long rushes on the bank. Never before had I anticipated such a monstrosity, nor do I ever wish to see another. A creature almost indescribable, though its general appearance is fixed in my mind's eye too indelibly for pleasant afterthought.

"The beast, fish or reptile, whatever species of God's creation it might be classed under, was a tawny greenish color, growing more definite toward the head. The body of the creature was seal shaped, apparently twenty feet long, and as thick as the carcass of the largest sized elephant. From this trunk sprung the most remarkable feature of the phenomenon, a long, curved, swan-like neck, large enough, apparently, to have taken a man in whole, terminated by a head and jaws similar to that of an immense boa constrictor, the eyes fishy yet possessing ferocity enough in their expression to make a man tremble. The back of the beast was deeply ridged, running from the base of the neck to the extreme end of the tail, and several inches deep. An immense tail, shaped something like an alligators, and three times longer, so it seemed, than the body, completed the tout ensemble of this wonderful anomaly. The creature navigated by feet resembling the fore feet of an alligator, and its progress on land was slow.

"'With all this combination of the terrible before me,' says our friend, 'it was not strange that I trembled, but before the frightened men had time to act, or I time to advise, the cause of our terror drew itself across the little island, out of sight, into the water beyond. It did not take us long to recover our senses, and as quickly leave the scene, though the shock to our nerves, and indeed to our belief in things possible and impossible, precluding anything like hard work.' "The above statement we have from the lips of the gentleman himself, and being duly vouched for, we have every reason to believe in its truth."

The only thing I don't like about the witnesses' description is the feet. Overall, he described a perfect Apatosaurus except for the alligator-like feet. An Apatosaurus had feet more akin to an elephant. However, this is only a problem if we limit the candidates to an Apatosaurus. A Nothosaurus, for example, was predominantly aquatic like a plesiosaur but had clawed, webbed feet, which a witness might compare to a alligator's from a distance. Dinosaurs from the Melanorosauridae family also had long necks with clawed feet.

Our next question is: was this monster a one-off? The answer is maybe, as similar creatures were seen in the area, but not specifically in the Wright River. There are legends of serpentine creatures in Catawba River in North Carolina. And, the Wright River actually intersects and feeds into the Catawba River.

The Catawba Native American tribe had legends of enormous snakes in the area—though they were just that, giant snakes, and did not possess legs. The Catawba River feeds into Lake Wylie, which rests between North and South Carolina. A monstrous serpent was seen there as recently as December of 2019 at Sunset Point.

The monsters of the Catawba River were notorious enough that local merchants sometimes used them in their advertising. The A. H. Hutchinson & Company wrote a fake newspaper account/advertisement that stated, "As the evening passenger train on the Carolina Central, which leaves Charlotte at 3:15, was passing Mt. Holly, yesterday, there was great excitement as they saw a monster sea serpent in the river which looked as large around as a small hogshead, and probably thirty or forty feet long. His green serpent-like eyes were blazing like fire as he lashed the water to foam."[9] Though it could sound exciting for a moment, the ending gives away the intent when it revealed that the monster was carrying a wooden sign instructing folks to buy their livery supplies from Hutchinson's store in Charlotte.

It's possible that the Catawba River monster found itself trapped in a man-made lake in the early 20th century. At that time, a series of hydroelectric dams were constructed across the Catawba, creating lakes like Lake Norman. Today the lake is home to the monster Normie, which in some accounts resembles the Loch Ness Monster while in others, it would seem to be a giant fish. Though I, of course, perpetuate the remnant dinosaur theory, those who like 1950's era B-movies can also go with the theory that the animal

---

[9] Hairr, *Monsters of North Carolina*, pp.97-98.

is a giant lizard mutated by radiation from the Maguire Nuclear Station, which resides on the lake's southern shore.

Whether the Wright River Monster is related to Normie and the Catawba River Monsters or not, the sighting seems to be a credible one.

Sources:

Hairr, John. *Monsters of North Carolina: Mysterious Creatures in the Tar Heel State.* Stackpole Books, 2013.

SOUTHERN SNAIK STORIES
Giant Florida Rattlesnake

Though you might think a giant rattlesnake story like this would be something more common to the Southwest, the South had the unwieldy critters as well, as evidenced in this article published in the *Elyria Republican* on November 14, 1878:

"Dumfounded at Seeing Such a Monster"

We are informed by Mr. Long, of Brevard county, Fla., that while driving his ox team near Ft. Drum, in that county, his ox shied and ran out of the road. Seeing something raise its head and a movement in the grass, Mr. Long, after stopping his team, went back to see what it was. Upon approaching the object he heard a great rustling and rattling, which convinced him that it was a rattlesnake, but he could not see it, because of the palmetto and high grass, until it threw itself into a coil and stood nearly as high as himself. He was almost dumfounded at seeing such a monster, and hastily retreated, but soon summoning up his courage, he advanced near enough to be within reach of the reptile with his long cow whip, which he knew how to handle.

"With this weapon he opened the conflict, which lasted nearly fifteen minutes, Mr. Long keeping out of reach of the snake, but still near enough to strike it with his cow-whip, which was about eighteen feet long. Finally Mr. Long began to feel sick and weak from the excitement, as well as from the musk emitted from the snake, and, putting in two[,] three or [more] rapid strokes with his whip, he retreated toward his cart, but fainted before he reached it. Upon coming to his senses again, he found that he had killed the snake. Mr. Long had no means of measuring its length but by his cow whip, which was 18 feet long, and the snake lacked about 2 1/2 feet of being as long as the whip. It had thirty-eight rattles and a button. He says it 'was as large around as a big blue bucket.' Mr. Long is one of the most reliable men of this section."

CHAPTER 8
ATTACK OF THE
FROGMAN
"A Curious Creature,
Half Man, Half Frog.."

I have a feeling that this article unfortunately exists to belittle the African American population more than anything else. Or, if not made up entirely, the writer took it upon himself to poke fun at the witnesses, who may have seen something similar to the Alligator Man from Palmetto, South Carolina, seen in 1892, ten years earlier. This story ran in the *Newberry Herald and News* on August 29, 1902.

IT HAS THEM GUESSING.
A CURIOUS CREATURE, HALF MAN,
HALF FROG.

It is Alleged to Have Come Out of Colonial Lake and Negroes and Superstitious Persons

Southerners & Saurians

are Much Disturbed - Expert Opinions, Including Some by Mr. Beeswax.

Negroes and superstitious folk are much concerned over the story that a hideous monster, half man and half frog, appeared on the bank of Colonial Lake a few minutes before 12 o'clock Thursday night and uttered strange and distressing cries. The frog man, as it has been dubbed, came out of the waters of Colonial Lake and remained on land probably a half hour before plunging again beneath the rippling wavelets. A fairly good view of the repulsive creature was obtained by William Harper, a colored truck driver and J.H. Thompson, a carpenter who lives on Smith street. There were others who could have enjoyed the pleasure of a close inspection of the frog man had they not excused themselves and gone away hurriedly when the saurian, or whatever you may choose to call it, crawled out of the lake.

"I was sitting on a bench on the east side of the lake," said Mr. Thompson yesterday to a Reporter for The Courier, "when I heard a mighty splashing in the water and a noise that sounded like this: Oough! O-o-o ugh! O-o-o ugh-how-ow! I wasn't' scured exactly, but I began to perspire. I watched the thing awhile, although I was prepared at any moment to go somewhere else. Finally, to my great surprise and - err, regret, the monster came ashore and laid down with another long O-O- O ugh! It was too horrible looking to describe. The head resembled that of a huge frog, the wide, protruding eyes burning with a lurid light. It had arms and shoulders like a man, but the body tapered down like a serpent. It was covered with large, greenish scales, and I should say it was at least eight feet long from head to tail. Its mouth was filled with crooked fangs, which it snapped together with a vicious click. I do not like to remain out late at night, so I started for home soon after the thing came ashore. I can't imagine what it is, where it came from, or whether it will ever show up again. But I'm entirely satisfied with the little knowledge I have of it. I wish now I'd never seen it. I'm afraid it's going to trespass on my dreams." "Boss, I cayn't give you no particlers about dat frog man," said Harper, the colored truck driver, to a Reporter for The News and Courier. "I didn't wait for no particlers. I was des siftin' and coolin' myself at Colonial Lake Thursday night, when I heard a mighty thrashing in de water. What in de debbil is dat, sez I to myself. My heart began to confabulate with mo' than its usual swiftness, when suddenly de horriblest lookin' critter I ever seen lunged out of de water and the next thing I knew I waz runnin'. Down Broad street I went a clippin', and I didn't have sense enough to stop until I collided wid de old Postoffice building. I thought I wuz both killed and injured, but when I got more calmer I realized that, while I wuz safe, it wuzn't necessary for me to go to Colonial Lake no more. Yas, sir, dat's

all I kno' about dat owdacious critter. See dis
bruise on my head? I got dat when I tried to run
over de old Postoffice building."

Scientists are ever interested in these
infrequent visitations to various seaports in
divers parts of the world of monsters from the
deep that defy classification and offer the widest
latitude for speculation and imagination.
Naturally, the frog-man of Colonial Lake will
come in for a share of local interest of the
speculative sort. What is its mission? A
Charleston man, whose knowledge is of
sufficient scope to enable him to discuss the
Colonial Lake mystery from the view point of a
scientist, was seen by a reporter for The News
and Courier. After listening to a description of
the frog-man he said:

"It is probably a megalosauria."

"What is a megalosauria?" asked the reporter,
respectfully.

"A megalosauria is a sub-order of dinosaurian
reptiles," he replied, "having the brain case
unossified in front and no ossified alisphenoids.
It has a short abdomen and an external chin. It
also has deciduous scales which indicate that it
is akin to the family of symbranchiate fishes.
The megalosauria is almost extinct, although,
according to science, it was very common in
these waters forty-two million years ago."

Not being wholly convinced that the frog-man
was a megalosauria, the reporter sought Mr.
Nathan Beeswax and asked for an expression of
opinion from him.

"Megalosauria! Bah!" exclaimed Mr. Beeswax, contemptuously. "Listen to me. This frog-man is nothing more nor less than a chilliandae, which is of the genus basommotophorous gastradods. Now hold that down if you have to choke it, and I'll tell you something about it. It has a bulimiform shell and a moveable lip that continues without interruption from the nose. These are the main characteristics of the chillinidea and they fit the frog-man exactly. No, it is not dangerous, but I don't think it will be given an ovation in Charleston."

The [African American population] were excitedly discussing the frog-man yesterday and Colonial Lake, as the place of resort, has ceased to attract them.

To return to the question posed at the beginning of this chapter, was the reporter making fun of a legitimate cryptid sighting just because one of the witnesses was African American? Or, did he simply make it all up to begin with? Whatever his angle was, it was in poor taste. The only thing in this story's favor is its being set in the home state of the Lizard Man, which has a fairly decent track record. But, this creature doesn't resemble the Lizard Man due to its having no bottom legs, only a tail. If the descriptions matched, we could just almost make a case for this creature. But, the odd description, coupled with the fact that no monsters have been reported in Colonial Lake since makes this a hard sell. The final nail in the coffin is the article's humorous ending, where various "scientists" spew out indecipherable "scientific facts" about the "Megalosauria" and the "chillianda."

In more recent years, there have been additional sightings of so-called Frogmen. That's what the strange, bipedal reptilians sighted in Loveland, Ohio, were dubbed in 1955. In May of that year, a businessman traveling down a road in the vicinity of the Little Miami River claimed he saw three reptilian beings standing erect. They were three to four feet tall and had heads like frogs.

The Loveland Frogmen returned in 1972 when one scuttled across the road in front of a policeman in his patrol car. A few weeks later, a separate officer saw the creature and shot it. As it turned out, it was an escaped iguana that had lost its tail...

CHAPTER 9
A MONSTER
ALLIGATOR
"...this specimen measured
twenty- two feet in length..."

The average length of an alligator can be anywhere from 9 to 15 feet. So, in the case of this 22 footer, we have a few possibilities. One, it was simply an exceptionally large variety of the modern-day alligator. Two, it was grossly exaggerated by the witnesses in terms of their size estimates. And my favorite: maybe it was a surviving Deinosuchus? But first, the story itself, as printed in the *New Philadelphia Times* on March 31, 1892, on page three:

SIZE OF ALLIGATORS,
They Are Quite Frequently Met with Sixteen Feet in Length.

I have seen numerous specimens of our saurian no longer than ordinary lead pencils; this was in the season of their hatching. I have also seen a few living specimens about sixteen feet in length, says a writer in the Century. In the autumn of 1875 I obtained for the late Effingham Lawrence, member of congress and commissioner from Louisiana to the Centennial exhibition, the dried skin of an alligator which, after at least fifteen inches had been cut from the snout and skull and ten inches from the end of the tail, still measured seventeen feet ten inches in length. Allowing more than six inches for shrinkage in drying, this monster of his kind alive must have measured more than twenty feet. He was killed in the lower part of Bayou Lafourche.

Probably the largest alligator ever seen in Louisiana was killed in a small lake on the plantation of H. J. Feltus in Concordia parish. According to the statement of Mr. Feltus, now of Baton Rouge, this specimen measured twenty-two feet in length. The great reptile had long been famous for miles around, having destroyed numbers of hogs and hounds owned in the neighborhood of his retreat, he had become so wary, from the number of ineffectual shots fired at him, as to be almost unap-proachable. Finally he fell victim to a long shot fired from a Mississippi rifle in the hands of Mr. Feltus, who had persevered in hunting him, having been the greatest loser by his depredations. The huge carcass of this reptile was towed to the bank by a boat. It required the strength of a pair of mules and a stout rope to

haul it ashore, where the measurement was
made, with the result above stated.

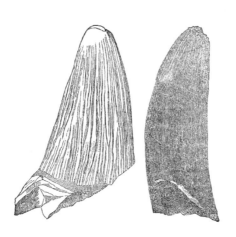

*ILLUSTRATION OF DEINOSUCHUS
FOSSIL TEETH C.1858.*

The Deinosuchus was essentially a giant,
Cretaceous crocodile which also had similarities to
the alligator. The Deinosuchus was discovered in
bits and pieces over many years—a complete
skeleton has yet to be found. First, two teeth were
found in Bladen County, North Carolina, in 1858.
Another large tooth was found in a neighboring
county a decade later in 1869. More pieces of the
puzzle were found in Willow Creek, Montana, in
1903. In the 1940s, the American Museum of
Natural History used fossils found in Big Bend
National Park, Texas, to reconstruct the skull.

Based on the skull, scientists thought the Deinosuchus may have reached a length of over 40 feet. However, modern evaluations have determined that the Deinosuchus was likely smaller than that and just had an oversized head. They estimated that the largest of the Deinosuchus might have reached 35 feet in length.

So, perhaps the specimen killed in Louisiana was a Deinosuchus not yet fully grown. Or, it could have simply been an oversized alligator.

SKULL RECONSTRUCTION AT THE AMERICAN MUSEUM OF NATURAL HISTORY C. 1954.

CHAPTER 10
RETURN OF THE
MISSISSIPPI MONSTER
"Flesh, Fish and Fowl."

The following article features another thrilling adventure of our friend, the Mississippi Monster, sporting a brand new design and having a few new abilities. After reading the article, published in the *St. Louis Republican* on October 7, 1877, I think you'll see why I didn't include it with the main entry on the Mississippi Monster from earlier.

FLESH, FISH, AND FOWL

A St. Louis reporter concocts the boss yarn

Mr. Jabez Smith is a well-to-do farmer on a small scale, whose place is situated in the bottom, 6 or 7 miles southeast of Cahokia. Mr.

Southerners & Saurians

Smith is a gentleman well known in his locality as an upright and thoroughly reliable citizen.

Mr. Smith's exciting account is to the effect that the strange River monster which has lately caused such a commotion on the Mississippi was on a Friday afternoon seen again, not near Memphis this time, but near Cahokia, and not in the water, but on land. It appears that at about 4 o'clock on Friday afternoon, Smith's boy was sent by his father to a pasture near a piece of woodland, about half a mile from the house, to drive home a brindle bull there confined. The bull, though small, is an extremely vicious animal, and young Smith, who appears endowed with a discretion beyond his age, took occasion to enter the pasture at a point some distance from the animal in order to test the bull's probable humor by shaking a stick at him, while leaving a margin for safe retreat should the ball prove ugly. This, as subsequently appeared, was a very fortunate circumstance for young Smith. Scarcely a moment had elapsed before the boy saw from his place of concealment the horrible solution to the mystery of the sound. From the edge of the woodlands there appeared a hideous head upon a swaying neck at least 20 feet in length. The head was that of a wolf or dog, save that there was a prolongation into a huge bill or horny jaws. This bill the monster opened at intervals, displaying a row of immense fangs upon each division, while as he opened it up on each occasion was admitted a hissing noise loud enough to be heard for a great distance. From the back of his head and down the neck descended a mane of coarse reddish hair. The monster retained its position for a moment or two, swaying its head gently back and forth, when its eyes fell upon the bull; then it at once showed signs of great excitement. It snorted fiercely, the hissing sound became almost continuous, and it would repeatedly open its immense jaws and snap them together with a sound like the report of a rifle. Its hesitation did not long continue. Maddened by the sight of the bull, the monster advanced at once and swiftly to the attack. Raising its head still higher it shot forward over the fence, and thence came over in swift, billowing undulations, the fence seeming no obstacle at all. As the animal entered the field its whole body could be distinctly seen. The great neck terminated in a body of somewhat less length, supported upon four short legs, armed with immense claws, though the motions of the animal seemed to resemble rather those of a snake than of a thing with legs. To the body was joined a tail quite as long as the neck, and terminating in a huge barb, apparently, as iron, and having the bright red color of a boiled lobster. The neck and entire body were sheltered in scales of a dark blue color, and as large as dinner plates. Most remarkable of all was a pair of huge membranous wings, which unfolded along the body on either side. The appearance of the great reptile was indescribably fearful and repulsive. It moved toward the bull, hissing loudly, and sweeping about the apparently dimmed animal in circles of decreasing extent.

The bull meanwhile retained his position, with lowered head and an occasional response to the hissing by a short bellow. As the monster swept about in circles the bull turned slowly, always keeping his front to the enemy. Suddenly the reptile raised its head to an immense height, opened its huge jaws, and darted forward.

The boy in the fence corner saw the shock of the encounter, and nothing more. Instantly there arose such a cloud of dust to almost conceal the combatants from sight. The ground shook as if with some internal convulsion. The air quaked with a co-mingled bellowing and roaring. Dimly discerned through the dust clouds could be seen portions of bull and reptile, and tufts of flying hair and chips of shattered scales. There could be heard the snap of the monster's jaws and the rattle of the bull's horns upon its mailed sides. Flashing here and there through the dingy nimbus, could be seen the blood - darts upon the reptile's tail as it sought to transfix its active opponent. It was a panorama of desperate battle, a volume of sound, a fierce encounter. The tide of the battle shifted insensibly to the vicinity of a huge oak stump which was near the center of the field. Then the boy saw the tail of the strange monster dart the great barb downward with the speed of a thunderbolt. There was a crack like the report of a cannon. The barb had again missed the bull, and this time encountered a harder substance. The boy, peering through the fence, gave a wild yell of satisfaction. The barb had buried itself in the stump! Then suddenly rearing its head again it unfolded for the first time the great membranous wings folded along its sides and rose in the air like a gigantic bat. With a wild, hoarse cry it darted upward to the height of hundreds of feet and took a southwesterly direction toward the Mississippi. A few moments later, from the direction of the distant river, came the sound of a tremendous splash and swash of waters, as though some heavy body had fallen into the river from a great height. The baffled monster had reached again his native element.

Cautiously the boy in the fence corner emerged from his retreat and approached the scene of the late encounter. The bull, nearly skinned, with but one ear and one horn remaining, stood there, weak but fearless still, stamping, lashing its sides with what little remained of its tail, and gazing in the direction where his antagonist had disappeared over the wood. There was hair enough on the ground to stuff the mattress with, and fragments of great scales were scattered about over an area of half an acre, while the great oak stump was absolutely riven in twain in the effort of the monster to release its forked tail from the tough wood. The boy flourished a stick at the bull and it started home quietly. It had been engaging in too grand a struggle to fool with the boy anymore.[10]

All I can say is, to whoever wrote this article, you had me until the monster flew off into the air... almost.

Sources:

Clark, Jerome. *Unnatural Phenomena: A Guide to the Bizarre Wonders of North America.* Santa Barbara, CA: ABC-CLIO, 2005.

---

[10] Jerome Clark, in his version reprinted in *Unnatural Phenomena,* has the following alternate ending paragraph: "Battered and bloodied the bull still stood, glaring angrily in the direction of his attackers escape. The ground was littered with scales and hair over half an acre. The oak stump was split in two from the creature's furious effort to free itself."

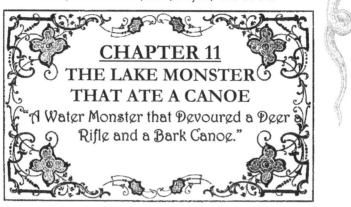

CHAPTER 11
THE LAKE MONSTER
THAT ATE A CANOE
"A Water Monster that Devoured a Deer
Rifle and a Bark Canoe."

*Y*ou can probably tell from the chapter title that
we have another real "stretcher" on our
hands here—"stretcher" being a term used by
the old-timers for stretching the truth. But who can
resist a good yarn about a lake monster that
potentially ate a canoe?

A Water Monster that Devoured a
Deer a Rifle and a Bark Canoe

From the Gadsden Ga. Times

I have noticed that in your paper has been
published imperfect descriptions of strange
water animals, of huge size, being seen in
Coosa. That, monsters of which we can find no
name in animal history were in that river many

years ago, there can be no doubt, if the tradition of one which was killed at the head of the Ten Islands, in St. Clair county be true. It is said that in 1816 and 1817, when North Alabama was being settled by the whites, there came to that county from Carolina, Jacob Green, the father of Abe Green, his son-in-law Mr. Wood, and perhaps Mr. Dill and Jeremiah Collins, father of the Rev. Jesse Collins, now of St. Clair, all of whom afterwards settled in that county. When they first came on their tour of inspection in search of a new home, they were attracted to Ft. Strother, on the Coosa, in consequence of its being the spot where Gen. Jackson, in the Creek War, had nine militia men and one Captain shot for mutiny in his army on its march into the Creek Nation, on the opposite side of the river. That place is but a few miles below the Ten Islands, and is opposite to some of them. They, as all other persons coming into the country at that time, brought with them firearms for their protection.

During their visit in search of homes they were induced to go on the islands to ascertain if they or any of them were of sufficient size to make a settlement. In order to reach them they procured Indian canoes, native bark of trees, in which to cross over the water onto the island. These bark canoes were very small crafts, only of sufficient size to carry one, or not more than two persons. Having prepared themselves for the inspection of the islands, they set out, and on approaching one, they saw a strange animal

of immense size and length, about the color of
a catfish, but more in the shape of a snake,
which seemed to have drifted up on the edge of
a small island, and was partly out of the water
making movements and contortions like it was
in the agonies of death. They approached it. It
was partly covered by the water and partly on
dry land, but was of such enormous size and
strange shape as to baffle all their ideas of such
animals or their names in the whole animal
kingdom; but that was certainly a water animal
of the snaky genus. After watching its
movements and holding a short consultation,
they determined, to kill it if bullets would do so.
They then approached more closely to it and
fired several rounds, until they discovered that
it was dead. Then they went to it for a close
examination to ascertain what it was, and
discovered, from the sharp protuberances and
unevenness of its body on one side, and the
evenness of the other, that there must be
something in it. When they discovered that they
had never seen or heard or read of such an
animal, they proceeded with their Tomahawks
and butcher knives to open it, and in doing so
to their utter amazement and surprise, they
found in it a bark canoe, the horns and skeleton
of a large deer, the skeleton of an Indian, also
an old rifle gun such as the Indians of that day
used, and a bow and arrows. From finding the
above-named articles in it, and their parents,
they concluded that some weeks previously an
Indian had killed a deer, put it into his canoe

and, while crossing the river, the monster had swallowed the canoe with the Indian, deer and other articles in it. The flush of the Indian and deer had been digested, but the canoe, the gun, the bow and arrows, and bones were so indigestible as to sicken the monster and so enfeeble it that it had floated to where they found it, and could not escape from them.

When others came to the country and this adventure was told to them, they were incredulous, and pronounce the whole story to be a lie. Those who destroyed the monster became more sensitive and declined speaking of it anymore, although they knew it to be true.

The story was published in the *Boonville Weekly Inquirer* on July 21, 1877. That these men encountered a lake monster isn't unbelievable at all in the context of this book's subject matter. What's unbelievable is when one actually thinks through the sequence of events. Could this creature have a mouth big enough to swallow a canoe with a man inside? Furthermore, could it even be fast enough? I think not.

CHAPTER 12
THE
LIVING
NIGHTMARE
"Sub Marine Monster."

I simply don't know what to make of this monster, which sounds like nothing I've ever heard of before. Furthermore, it seems more like a grotesque creature dreamed up in the mind of a 1980s horror screenwriter rather than something an 1880s newspaperman would conjure up. Several variations of the article describing the monster were printed, but the best and the most in-depth was found in the *Florida Agriculturist* on November 5, 1884:

SUB MARINE MONSTER.

STRANGE FISH OR REPTILE CAUGHT IN THE MISSISSIPPI RIVER.

Southerners & Saurians

A strange marine monster was brought to this city yesterday, says the Nashville American, and will be put on exhibition this week, in a building near the square. Bill Orley and Nick Moley, two old fishermen, caught it in the river just above the water-works a few days ago, and since that time it has been fastened securely to the river bank by stakes driven around its body, in addition to which it is hog-chained by the tail to the bank.

When seen in this position yesterday it appeared to be about the size of a Newfoundland dog. It had webbed feet, that were attached to the body by legs without joints. Its body and back, except the stomach, is covered with large, diamond-shaped bony scales. The long, coarse yellow hair growing out of these scales and the skin, which bulges out in welts between the scales, hangs together like that on an Angora goat, and is as coarse and tough as coconut skin fibers. But its mouth is well worth a detailed description. It is certainly the most hideous opening that is developed in the countenance of any animal extant or told about by scientists.

It is about the size of that of a large alligator, but shaped like that of a shovel-nosed shark, being very blunt at the end. And the teeth! There are no less than three rows of them in both the upper and lower part of the mouth. The teeth are all jagged, the upper rows fitting into the lower rows, and the jaws working laterally, so as to make the teeth grind to powder everything that falls into them.

The reptile, devil-fish, or whatever it is, crawls sideways like a crab, and its eyes are placed one above the other in the top of the skull, and bulge out like pegs on a hat rack. There are no lids to the eyes, so that the animal cannot wink, but it pops its eyes in and out of the sockets so fast when the monster is angry that the noise made by this working of the eyes is similar to the sound made by a cow's feet when the animal is wading in soft, deep mud. The tail is shaped like that of a beaver's and is covered with warts of various sizes, the smallest being about the size of a dime, and the largest about the size of a half dollar. Each one of these warts seem to possess the power of moving separately from the other, and when the whole mass gets to working it is something frightful to behold. It has rather more the appearance of a swarm of bees hanging from the limb of a tree, than anything else, and is altogether the most sickening sight imaginable.

The whole animal is covered with a thick green slime, which seems to ooze out of its body, and especially its tail, where it seems to originate from the center of small mouths or openings, one of which is the center of each of the warts mentioned. When prodded with a stick the animal snaps its eyes, grinds its teeth, and each particular hair stands on end, and every inch of its body seems to writhe, squirm, and jerk on its own account and in the manner and direction that seem to give it most comfort. The tongue is forked and black, and darts in and out like that of a sea-serpent.

The two fishermen who captured it have followed this means of making a livelihood for many years. It seems that the existence of this animal has been known to them and a number of old rivermen in this city for a number of years. They say it has made its abode under a high bank on the left-hand side as you go up the river in a place suitable for such a terrible, uncanny looking thing to live without much hesitation. They have been much annoyed by this reptile and have been put to a great deal of experience in repairing their lines, as fish-hooks seemed only to whet its appetite. As if by instinct it knew when and where the lines were set and would go to devour the bait and destroy the lines, which it did almost every night.

But lately a new method was resorted to for dealing with this monster, which resulted in its capture, to the great delight, as well as astonishment, of both the fishermen. Instead of resorting to the old method of fishing, they procured a long, heavy clothes-wire, and stretched it midway across the river. It was attached at the end of a ten gallon keg, that acted as a buoy. To anchor it down an old iron cog-wheel was used. About sixty feet from the shore the bait was set in a large steel trap and let down. It was not long before it was gobbled, as a fisherman, who was looking after his other lines, discovered.

The keg was seen bobbing up and down, and suddenly disappeared altogether. They commenced to haul in their line, and came very near upsetting their skiff. The reptile by this time was furious, and lashed the waters into a white foam. It was found impossible to land it with the boat, and it took two hours to pull the beast out on dry land. An old fish-net was promptly thrown over it, and secured by driving stakes around the outside. The monster bit, snapped, and struggled all night to free itself, until finally, when it was exhausted, five men brought it across the river in a flatboat, and left it at an old sawmill, just below the water-works, where his satanic majesty now reposes. There the reptile has since been viewed by the curious hundreds of people who have been going there to see the brute.

A separate article published earlier in the *Goshen Times* on August 07, was shorter but offered a few additional/alternate details such as that, "The teeth are all short, diamond-shaped, jagged, the upper rows fitting into the lower rows, and the jaws working laterally so as to make the teeth grind to powder everything that falls into them." Another portion added more details to the eyes, stating:

...its eyes are placed one above the other in the top of the skull, and bulge out like the pegs on a hat-rack. There are no lids to the eyes so that the animal cannot wink, but it pops its eyes in and out of the sockets so fast when the monster is angry that the noise made by this working of the eyes is similar to the sound made by a cow's feet when the animal is walking in soft deep mud.

There were never any follow-ups on the strange submarine monster. If it was real, I have to wonder if it was some sort of heretofore unknown crustacean?

CHAPTER 13
MONSTER MOSQUITOS
"Averasboro Gallinipper."

On the banks of the Cape Fear River once sat the town of Averasboro, which could turn into a particularly wild place whenever timber-rafters passed through. In the mid-1850s, 13 of the town's 14 buildings sold liquor if that tells you anything. In one of the taverns, the "skeleton" of a monster mosquito hung from the rafters. Insects, of course, don't have skeletons, and it was really just the skeleton of a large bird with the beak removed and replaced with a carved bone resembling a needle. The monstrosity was meant to represent the Averasboro Gallinipper, a species of giant mosquito alleged to haunt the river.

The Gallinipper could be considered just as folkloric as Rhinelander's Hodag except that it actually correlated to local Native American legends. According to Tuscarora myth, North

Southerners & Saurians

Carolina was the birthplace of the mosquito. The first of its kind was a giant called Ro-tay-yo that sprang from underneath the grounds of the Neuse River.

This man-sized mosquito was recorded by the Tuscarora chief Elias Johnson in the nineteenth-century. Johnson wrote, "It flew about with vast wings, making a loud noise, with a long stinger, and on whomsoever it lighted it sucked out all the blood and killed him. Many warriors were destroyed in this way, and all attempts to subdue it were in vain."[11]

Eventually the monster flew north, to Onondaga in present-day New York State. A warrior named Tarenyawagon chased the creature all the way over to the Great Lakes and killed it with an arrow. From its blood was spawned the smaller mosquitos we know today.[12]

It's unknown if workmen in 1850's Averasboro picked up on the Tuscarora legends or if they simply made up tales of their own. Whatever the case, they claimed that the swamps were infested by mosquitos as large as birds!

Some of the men seemed to sincerely believe in these oversized bugs, while others just enjoyed telling tall tales about them. One of the more famous stories about the creatures was unearthed by historian Malcolm Fowler. In 1855, two groups

---

[11] Hairr, *Monsters of North Carolina*, pp.83.

[12] This wasn't the only Native American tribe to speak of a giant mosquito monster. So too did a tribe near the Great Salt Lake in Utah.

of workmen were cutting timber deep in the forest along Beaverdam Swamp. One group was from Chatham County and the others were from the town of Averasboro. The Chatham County men bet that Red Saunders, the toughest man in their group, could lie facedown shirtless for one hour and endure the mosquitos without flinching.

According to the legend, Saunders lasted fifty-five minutes before the Gallinipper came calling. Red Billy Avera saw it first and cried out, "What is that!?" Though Avera pointed to the sky, no one could see any monster mosquitos. But then Saunders cried out in pain—as if bitten by a giant insect.

THE STRAND MAGAZINE'S *DEPICTION OF A GIANT MOSQUITO C.1909.*

Saunders lost his bet, though it's likely the Gallinipper wasn't to blame. Supposedly someone threw a hot coal on his back!

Southerners & Saurians

While the giant mosquitos spoken of by the timber workers are most certainly mythical, one still has to wonder about those from Native American legend...

Sources:

Hairr, John. *Monsters of North Carolina: Mysterious Creatures in the Tar Heel State.* Stackpole Books, 2013.

CHAPTER 14
MESSAGE INSIDE
A MONSTER
"A Sensational Finding of a Hideous
Monster in Tallulah River."

*Y*ou've heard about a message inside of a bottle, but what about a message inside of a monster? This story was printed in the *Athens Banner* on May 17, 1891, on page five.

A WHAT "IS-IT?"
A SENSATIONAL FINDING OF A
HIDEOUS MONSTER
IN TALLULAH RIVER.
A Thrilling Account of the Affair by
'Pegwood'—The Last Work of Reporting he
Ever Did—A Queer Arrival.

A hideous monster.

There has been a queer animal caught near Tallulah Falls.

Pegwood was an eyewitness, and wrote the account of the capture of the beast given below. It is the last reporting Pegwood ever did, his death occurring soon afterward.

The story is an interesting one, and was published in the Toccoa News as follows:

The people of this vicinity are very much excited over a wonderful monster washed out of Tallulah river by the last few weeks of copious rain, the river being, at least six feet higher than it ever before has been known to be.

Yesterday, reports reached our town of a terrible monster being washed out of Tallulah River, near which is known as Hinckle's Hole and left on dry land. Not considering the report altogether reasonable, we, with several persons, hastily made our way to the spot to fully investigate the monster. On arriving at the place we found—though there had been some slight deviations from the truth—that the essentials of the report were true. Quite a crowd had gathered at the spot to view the monster. We found that it measured 27 feet instead of 40, which had been reported. The animal seemed to be stunned by being rapidly washed over the rocks, and cliffs in the river, and being hurled through timber, brush and mud, where it was thrown against a large fallen tree, and jammed so tight it could not escape.

The river being very swift at this point receded fast and left the monster on dry land. The animal's head is larger in proportion than its body, and somewhat resembles an alligator; but its head is much broader. For several hours its jaws would automatically open and close with a vicious snap which made the cold chill creep over the spectators. A pole as large as a man's leg being put in his mouth, was instantly snapped into flinders, and on being examined gradually turned black. The green froth from the monster's mouth turned flint rocks to a bright scarlet color, and caused them to smoke with a smell resembling sulphur. The body of the monster resembled a rattlesnake, except a row of large fins which extended from its neck to within 15 inches of its tail, and a row of short legs of paddles on either side of its belly. Its tail was in the shape of a ram's horn and equally as hard. After fully examining the monster a Winchester rifle being on hand, a 48 caliber ball was planted between its eyes, which glanced off the same as if it had been shot against an iron clad gunboat. Finding a ball would not penetrate its skull, another spot was aimed at, its eye. The moment the ball struck it, it squirmed over with a terrible groan, lashed its tail against a huge oak and expired. Major Rembert, who, years ago, had a summer home on the cliffs overlooking Tallulah river, and who kept a lot of fish traps in the river, often saw this monster in the river, but was unable to see it in a sufficient shape to fully describe it. After it was dead and no danger of a near approach, it was suggested the skin be taken off, which with considerable trouble, was accomplished, Then someone suggested we cut the monster open in order to see something of his digestive powers and to the horror of all, we found a No. 8 pair of boots, a nice suit of clothes, coat and vest, about half worn, a Waterbury watch, a bottle of whiskey and a deck of cards, one set brass cuff buttons with the initials T. D. Some of the boys said it was a town dude the monster had swallowed. There were no papers in the pockets except part of a slip, on which you could faintly see penciled: Special from Toccoa to the Constitution, "A Monster Found in the Tallulah River."

This is all we could decipher as to who it was as his flesh and bones had been digested. There was also a sign board inside the monster which doubtless washed down the river from the Falls as it read 'Grand View Hotel'. Three ox yokes, several plow stocks, gate posts and various other farming tools not digested.

The hide will be stuffed with saw dust, and can be seen during the summer at the Grand View Hotel after which it will be sent to the World's Fair.

Bet this story had you going until the note inside read "A Monster Found in the Tallulah River." However, I felt the story was a little fishy to begin with due to similarities to the Mississippi Monster story from 1877, in which a beached up monster is shot at (but not killed) by observers. They're similar enough to make me wonder if this story was a regurgitated version of that one, changing the monster's description and the names of the witnesses.

CHAPTER 15
OUT OF PLACE
ANACONDA
IN LOUISIANA
"Monster Reptile."

nother facet of cryptozoology, outside of heretofore undiscovered animals and prehistoric survivors, is that of out of place animals. Essentially, a known species of animal popping up outside of its usual environment, sometimes on another continent altogether. This story doesn't present a remnant dinosaur, but what appears to be an exceptionally large Anaconda found in Louisiana. The story was printed in the *Philadelphia Inquirer* on November 1, 1877, on page three.

MONSTER REPTILE.

A Snake Thirty Feet Long Killed In Louisiana

We were yesterday informed by Mr. Smith, living on Quapaw bay, that while he and his son

Southerners & Saurians

William, aged thirteen years, were out in the woods on Monday afternoon last, driving their cattle their attention was attracted by the bleating of a calf some distance from them. Thinking probably that the poor animal had bogged, they started to its assistance.

They had gone a short distance down the bayou when they discovered a yearling in the coils of a huge snake, the body of which was suspended from the limb of a black gum tree about twenty feet from the ground, and which projected from the bank immediately over the water. Mr. Smith and his son were almost terror stricken at the sight, and stood speechless for several moments, unconsciously watching the movements of the huge reptile as he twined himself around the already dead body of the yearling, and at every coil of the snake they could hear the bones of the calf break.

After coiling itself around the lifeless form of the yearling and crushing every bone in its body, the serpent let loose its hold from the tree, and dropped down alongside its victim, and began licking it all over, preparatory, it is supposed, to swallowing it. About this time Mr. Smith recovered his senses, and after watching the monster snake open its capacious mouth several times, he fired on it with his rifle, striking it on the head, and was quickly followed by his son, who discharged a double barreled gun loaded with buckshot. Both reloaded as quickly as possible, and again fired on his snakeship. In the meantime, the reptile had coiled itself into a huge mass, and was making a hissing sound that could be heard fully one hundred yards, and was protruding its forked tongue several feet.

1897 ENGRAVING OF ANACONDA.

Southerners & Saurians

After discharging about a dozen volleys each, Mr. Smith and his son succeeded in dispatching one of the largest snakes ever seen in Louisiana, and, probably, in North America. It measured thirty-one feet in length, and the body measured, ten feet from the head, thirty inches in circumference, and about the center of the body forty-two inches. It has a regular succession of spots, black and yellow alternating, extending from its head to its tail, while either side is a deep purple. Mr. Smith has no idea what kind of snake it is, but thinks it must be of the boa constrictor species. No doubt this snake has for many years inhabited that section of country and depredated upon the young calves and animals that came within its reach. The skin of this huge snake has been preserved, and will be sent to Shreveport and put on exhibition.— Shreveport Times, 27th

SOUTHERN SNAKE STORIES
Battle with a Sea Serpent

Stories of Sea Serpents in the Gulf Coast were fairly common throughout the 19th Century, but this one from *The Daily Morning Astorian* on November 13, 1887, is particularly exciting:

THE SEA SERPENT.

WASHINGTON, Nov. 7. Information has reached this city that a sea serpent or an unknown marine monster was shot in the Gulf of Mexico, but on account of its immense size only the head could be secured. The head will soon be in possession of the National Museum, there to be "sat on" by the scientific sharps. To Captain James P. Hare, who is in charge of the Trinity Show Lightship, off the Louisiana coast, belongs the honor of securing this prize. He has relatives in this city, and to them he has written a very interesting letter describing his encounter with the monster of the sea. He says that while his ship was lazily rolling on the ground swell, one of the seamen came to him and told him that he had seen a strange object in the sea, a couple of cable-lengths from the ship.

The Captain, with the aid of a pair of powerful glasses, saw, to use his own words, "As hideous a creature as ever the human eye rested upon. The first casual glance convinced me that, although from boyhood following the precarious vicissitudes of a seaman's life, and having visited all the prominent waters of the globe, and naturally seeing many strange inhabitants of the sea and land, I found it impossible to name or classify this monster in view."

Determined to investigate further, the Captain called for a volunteer crew and a boat was immediately manned. In addition to harpoons and axes, Captain Hare took his rifle and fifty rounds of ball cartridges. When they got within fifteen yards of their prey the boat stopped and Hare fired.

"Simultaneously with the sharp crack of the rifle and the thud of the striking bullet," he writes, "it suddenly reared its head high and began lashing the water with intense fury. Never have I seen such fury displayed by any creature exhibited. Its motions were so rapid and furious that it was impossible for the eye to retain its form. All that was distinguishable was a huge, dark, writhing mass, surrounded by seething foam, into which the water was lashed by the stricken and enraged monster."

In a few minutes the Captain fired another shot, which only seemed to further enrage the beast. By this time the blood was spurting from a number of wounds in the head, and the surrounding waters were dyed a deep crimson. Suddenly it turned, and with distended jaws, which showed its huge, tusk-like teeth, commenced to approach the boat. The crew stood ready for the attack. Hare realized that it was a fight to the death, and the chances were even if not in their adversary's favor.

He threw out four empty water-breakers, hoping thereby to distract its attention long enough to enable him to strike a vital part. The ruse worked to a certain extent. The sea-serpent chewed up the breakers one after another, and the Captain kept up a constant fusillade, but without being able to reach a vital spot. "As it reached the side of the boat," he writes, "it slowly raised its hideous head, erected its neck, and with wide-extended jaws it seized the side of the gunwale of our boat and crushed it as easily as though it was made of glass. The crew rained in blow after blow in rapid succession with their axes and hatchets. The harpooner thrust his keen weapon to the hilt in its eyes, while I shot into its quivering body ball after ball. It was not long that this strange and curious battle continued. After a few spasmodic tremblings the animal suddenly, with one convulsive jerk that carried away the side of the boat, fell with a splash along side, a huge dead, repulsive mass. As it slowly settled beneath the surface of the water we hastily attached a tow-line and tried by every effort in our exhausted condition to secure it for other and more scientific investigation.

Although we went to work with a will I soon found that the strong southerly current, together with the cumbersome body of the monster, our almost dismantled boat and our exhaustion was rapidly setting us to leeward and on the shoals, and being now some distance from the ship and night fast setting in, I was most reluctantly compelled to order the reptile cut adrift. But before we did so we severed its head from its huge body, which we soon saw disappear in the dark water."

Captain Hare says he cannot form any idea of the creature's length. At no time did he see more than forty or fifty feet exposed, and how much more was submerged is only problematical. Its color was a rusty-black on top, fading to a yellowish-white on the under part.

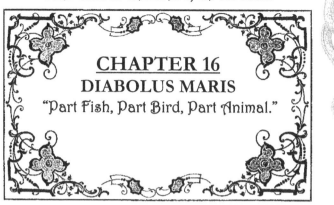

CHAPTER 16
DIABOLUS MARIS
"Part Fish, Part Bird, Part Animal."

T his story, printed in the *New York World* on August 09, 1896, would seem to be a hoax. Though the strange little cryptid, Diabolus Maris ("Sea Devil"), has gone on to become semi-famous in Fortean circles for its odd appearance, nothing like it has ever been reported since.

PART FISH, PART BIRD, PART ANIMAL

Sea serpents are becoming too common, and when Florida people decided to produce a marine monster the serpent family was ignored and the Diabolus Maris was produced.

The picture which is presented by the Sunday World was made from a drawing sent to the Kansas City Journal by Capt. George Bier, of the United States Navy. The animal was caught off the coast of Florida, at Malanzas Inlet, in seventy-two feet of water.

It was caught on a hook and line, and when dragged aboard the boat was full of fight. In order to preserve the strange monster it was found necessary to kill it, for it was so vicious that it could not be handled,

THE DIABOLUS MARIS.

A STRANGE BEAST.

This remarkable relic of the antediluvian monsters seemed to be part bird, part fish and part animal. Capt. Bier described it as follows:

"It has no scales, although it can swim. A portion of its body is covered with hair, and when it wants to fly it inflates two windbags behind its wings. This inflation is through its gills, which are situated on its breast. It stands upright on its feet, which are shaped like hoofs. Its face and body are more human-like than anything else, and its mouth is like that of a raccoon, garnished with two rows of teeth. It stood about twenty inches high and strutted like a rooster."

After its capture the monster was christened Diabolus Maris, and was transferred to Tampa, Fla., where it has since been on exhibition. Naturalists who have seen it can find no other name for it and its like has never been seen before.

Some fish have fins that resemble wings, and can be used for flying, but fish do not wear hair. The presence of legs argues that it is not a fish, and its ability to live under water and the gills prove that it is not a bird.

There's a very good chance that the Diabolus Maris corpse was real, but that it was simply several mummified and/or taxidermied sea creatures stitched together to create a new animal. These were called a Jenny Haniver, after the mythical sea creature. Usually they were the carcass of a ray that had been modified by the human hand. It would then be dried, resulting in a mummified alien-looking figure.

Though a few cryptozoologists have speculated that the creature might have been a baby pterodactyl of some sort, the previous explanation is still the most likely.

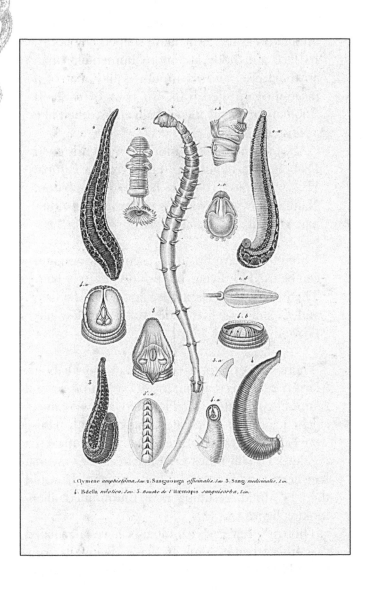

1. Clymene amphistoma, Sav. 2. Sanguisuga officinalis, Sav. 3. Sang. medicinalis, Lin.
4. Bdella nilotica, Sav. 5. Bouche de l'Hæmopis sanguisorba, Lin.

CHAPTER 17
ATTACK OF THE
GIANT LEECHES
The Legend of "Tlanusi'yi."

*e*arlier we covered a giant mosquito in the form of the Averasboro Gallinipper. But, that wasn't the only monster insect from North Carolina. At the junction of the Hiwassee and Valley Rivers in Cherokee County used to be a Native American settlement called "Tlanusi'yi" which roughly translates to "the Leech Place." But, as you can guess, these were no ordinary leeches.

According to tribal lore, the Cherokee were warned by another tribe of the monster before they even settled there. These people advised the Cherokee not to cross the river, for in it lived a monster leech that would eat them up. After settling there, the Cherokee came to believe that the beast lived in an underwater cavern, and that when it surfaced the water would boil and foam. The same thing would happen at a spot two miles away on the Nottely River. Therefore the Cherokee believed an underground tunnel connected both spots that the leech frequented.

Though it spent most of its time underwater, the gigantic leech was sometimes spotted sunning itself on a rock ledge at the junction of the Hiwassee and Valley Rivers. And it wasn't friendly either. One tale told of two men spotting the creature there one day, sunning itself as usual. They claimed that it had red and white stripes along its body. What happened next is so unwieldy it can undoubtedly only be folklore. According to the story, the monster became so agitated that the twisting of its tail created a wave that washed both men into the river.

The monster used the same maneuver on a young Cherokee man who tried to kill the beast, and he was washed into the river too.

GIANT LEECH OF THE AMAZON.

Though the beast creating waves and whirlwinds with its tail must be purely folkloric, is it possible that the legend was based on an actual creature? In the world of science, the largest recorded leech is the giant Amazon leech (*Haementeria ghilianii de Filippi*). The creatures grow to a length of eighteen inches at the longest, and have a six-inch-long proboscis. Could one of these leeches have found their way into North America, or was the beast really as large as the Cherokee described it? If so, it would have to be a heretofore undiscovered species that has since gone extinct.

If we are to consider prehistoric candidates that survived into the modern era, there is a monstrous worm called the bristle worm. Like a leech, it lived underwater but measured about three feet long. It also had a nasty pair of jaws.

HIWASSEE DAM C.1940s.
LIBRARY OF CONGRESS.

Today the giant leech monster is no longer seen, and the Hiwassee Dam was formed at the site of its old haunts in 1940.

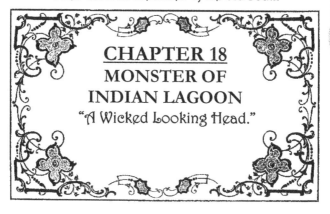

CHAPTER 18
MONSTER OF
INDIAN LAGOON
"A Wicked Looking Head."

I n Florida exists a 121-mile long brackish lagoon
called the Indian River Lagoon system. It is so
named for the Ais Native American tribe and
extends southward from the Ponce de Leon inlet
in Volusia County down to the Haulover Canal and
along the western shore of Merritt Island. The
tropical lagoon is the perfect abode for a swamp
monster, and yet it has none. At least none that stay
there permanently. But in 1895, it did have a rather
large serpentine visitor, possibly a sea monster that
snaked its way up through one of the tributaries
and into the lagoon. A story printed in the March
29, 1895 edition of the *Atlanta Constitution* tells of
a frightening encounter in the lagoon.

MAMMOTH SEA SERPENT.
Wicked-Looking Reptile Appears in the Indian

Southerners & Saurians

River at Titusville, Fla.

From The St. Louis Globe-Democrat.

For a month there have been reports that there was an immense sea serpent in the Indian river, which showed a disposition to fight when molested, but these reports, up to yesterday, were regarded as the product of the overwrought imaginations of rivermen. Yesterday, however, the truth of these reports was confirmed by the appearance of the monster off this place. About 9 o'clock yesterday people on the wharf waiting for the steamer saw a great black object resembling a hogshead floating in the river about seventy-five yards from shore. The object appeared to be lifeless, and those who saw it thought it was a piece of wreckage. Captain Simmonds and Fred White resolved to investigate. They took a boat and rowed toward the object. When within twenty-five feet of the object the men were surprised to see it show signs of life, and a moment later were horrified when a wicked looking head, with basilisk eyes, was darted at them with a hiss that could be heard half a mile. The men backed water for life, and the monster began to uncoil itself and move. It went through the water like a snake, was about sixty feet in length, and its body in the thickest portion was as large as a barrel. The head of the monster was similar to that of a snake, and for about six feet along its back there appeared to be a row of fins. The body of the reptile tapered gradually to a pointed tail. The monster moved down the river in plain sight of hundreds of people who were on the wharf. As it passed the men who had guns began shooting at it, and the reptile resented these shots by erecting its head six feet or more and emitting several hisses. Then it sunk below the surface and was seen no more.

Captain Simmonds and Fred White, who went out to inspect the object, were so overcome when they reached shore that restoratives had to be applied. They say they saw rows of immense teeth in the reptile's mouth, and that its breath was most noxious. About midday a steamer arrived from the south and reported passing the monster thirty miles below Titusville. The appearance of the monster has demoralized tourist travel on the Indian river and the house boats of the wealthy northerners have been deserted.

INDIAN RIVER SCENE C.1898.
LIBRARY OF CONGRESS.

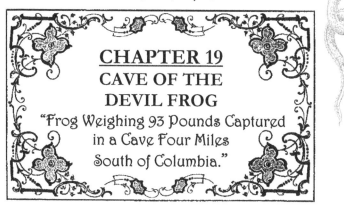

CHAPTER 19
CAVE OF THE DEVIL FROG
"Frog Weighing 93 Pounds Captured in a Cave Four Miles South of Columbia."

I 'm skeptical of the following story due to the fact that it came on the heels of Mark Twain's 1865 story "The Celebrated Jumping Frog of Calaveras County." In that story, two men bet upon whose frog can jump the farthest. One of the men cheats the other by making his frog swallow lead. The following story about a 93 pound giant frog was published in the *Nashville Union and American* on March 14, 1869:

A Frog Weighing 93 Pounds Captured in a Cave Four Miles South of Columbia — Great Excitement.

From the Columbia Herald.

Southerners & Saurians

We received the following letter late yesterday evening, at the hands of Mr. Lem. Matthews, who vouches for every word in the letter, and from his well-known integrity, and that of his brother, we feel not the least hesitancy in saying that it is just as they represent:

Near Indian Camp Spring, Wednesday, March 10, 1869. - Mr. Horsley - Having a large cave within a short distance of my house - and it having excited the curiosity of my two little boys, aged respectively eleven and thirteen years, they ventured this morning to explore its hidden wonders. With torches in hand they proceeded to the distance of about one hundred yards from the entrance, when they were terribly startled by the appearance of a monster frog, as large as a hogshead, as they said, when they came running up to me at my house.

Having seen so much in imagination, when young, and possessing a considerable degree of curiosity - I was determined to see for myself what it was. I went to the residence of Mr. W.D. Matthews to get assistance in exploring, and found several neighbors, J.W.B. Thomas, Richard McCanless, Geo. Dixon, John Due, and Sol. Porter there, who were eager to go right away, as their curiosity seemed as great or greater than mine.

In a short time we fixed up three torches, procured some candles, and a lantern, we proceeded on our voyage of discovery.

Having arrived at the mouth of the cave, the torches were soon lighted, but some hesitancy seemed to be shown by all as to who should go first.

Mr. Thomas led the van into the damp cavern, whose gloominess produced a chilling melancholy, (and one of the party was extremely anxious that they should retrace their steps,) but the indomitable Thomas and daring Mathews and Porter prevented, by telling the party that "we can whip out all the frogs in creation."

We wended our way slowly to the place my sons saw the frog, and sir, I do say to you, without exaggeration, that the frog was not near as large as when my children saw it, but it is undoubtedly the largest specimen I have ever seen or heard of before in this or any other State.

We advanced to within about twenty feet and halted. It was then sitting with its side to us, and when all of the torches were brought up it turned slowly around facing us - and such a hideous sight! I never before beheld. Its eyes, as they glistened in the torch light, made such an impression upon me, and in fact upon the whole party, that we trembled as if in the presence of a real demon, for in all my imaginations of the appearance of a demon, I must acknowledge that I never conceived of anything that would be calculated to fill the mind with such a horror as this.

We stood in the position we had first taken for some time. Mr. Matthews threw a small stone towards the frog, it rolled and struck him lightly. It bowed or ducked its head twice towards the ground in succession and made a leap towards us; and if I tell you he leaped ten feet I do not believe that I would miss it six inches. As soon as it struck the ground an instant retreat was simultaneously agreed upon, without consultation. The torches were thrown to the ground and in an instant Egyptian darkness reigned and a struggle was made to gain the entrance. The noise and excitement was intense amongst the little boys who attended us, and above the din of confusion the voice of Dick McCanless could be heard: "Is a frog bite poisonous?"

Mr. Porter having some matches the candles were soon lighted, and with the light came back the courage of the little boys. An advance of a few steps brought us in sight of the monster again. A plan for its capture was soon determined upon. Mr. Matthews sent to his house for a large goods box, which soon after arrived. The box was dragged in and the top removed. The box was pushed by Messrs. Dixon and Due towards the frog; Mr. Mathews using the top as a shield, succeeded in getting behind the frog, and by throwing stones at it for some little time, made it change its position to a place near the wall. The box was then pushed slowly up and covered it; the top was slipped down, the box was turned over and secured by a few nails, and the prize was ours. Right glad did we all feel at our success, and with high hearts we commenced the work of dragging the

box out of the cave, which we accomplished
after much labor; and we lifted it into a cart and
started for the residence of Mr. W.D. Mathews,
to have it weighed, as I had no balances that
would draw enough at my house. A rope was
tied around the box and the frog and box were
weighed together. The frog was then turned out
into a chicken coop and the box weighed and
showed that the frog weighed exactly ninety-
three pounds.

I will be willing to make an affidavit of this fact
before any justice of the peace in Maury county.
Those present and saw the weighing can attest
to this. It is, I dare say, as rare a curiosity as was
ever found in our county before. Mr. Mathews
measured it while it was in a sitting posture and
its height was exactly three feet four inches. Its
eyes, as near as we could guess, were two and
one-half inches in diameter. The color of the
breast or belly was a dark yellow, while its back
was a dark green, and apparently mossy, around
its neck are two distinct red and one dark stripe.
From the center of the head, or rather
commencing from the top center of the nose
there are apparently a thousand small light
stripes springing out from a common center like
rays of light. Its feet are of large proportions and
are perfectly black.

I laid claim to it, as my boys were first to
discover it, which claim was not objected to by
any of the party who went with me. If nothing
happens to it, I will bring it to Columbia next
week and give your town people an opportunity

of seeing something worth seeing. I will probably come to town on Tuesday and it will remain at Mr. W.D. Mathews' until that time. I would like very much for you to see this frog before its moved.

- A.P.N Matthews

The largest frog currently known to man is the African Goliath Frog, which can reach the size of a rabbit. Or, rather, it's the largest frog still in existence today. The prehistoric past sported the aptly named *Beelzebufo ampinga* (or, "lord of the flies"). This giant frog was still nowhere near as big as the three-footer described in the newspaper article, though. It was only a little larger than the current African Goliath Frog and is thought to have weighed ten pounds tops.

*BEELZEBUFO AMPINGA,
PENCIL DRAWING BY N. TAMURA.*

Considering that the animal lived during the late Cretaceous, it is thought that the frog could have devoured small dinosaurs due to its larger than normal mouth! The first fossil remains were discovered by David W. Krause in 1993. Over the next 17 years, 75 more fossil fragments were found, allowing researchers to reconstruct the creature in 2010. It was unveiled at the Stony Brook University Medical Center in 2010 as the "Frog from Hell."

To entertain the tale from 1869, perhaps what the men encountered was a larger specimen of the prehistoric devil frog? As it is, very little is known about the creature compared to other prehistoric life forms. Of course, there is a greater possibility that the story was created as a perfect tall tale with a nice southern flavor to it.

As it is, there aren't a lot of other frog cryptids to lend this story much credibility aside from the Loveland Frogmen, mentioned earlier in Chapter 8. However, those creatures were bipeds (who also possessed magic wands in one variation of the sighting).

Though the animal in this story sounds like it could be a prehistoric monster frog, more likely than not, the 93-pound frog was just a figurative "whopper" rather than a literal one.

Southerners & Saurians

SOUTHERN SNAIK STORIES
Treasure in the Belly of a Monster!

From the August 29, 1889 edition of the *Reno Weekly Gazette and Stockman:*

The story comes from Leighton, Miss., that John Davis, while hunting the other day, shot and killed a snake of the moccasin variety that measured 16 feet 5 inches in length and 21 inches in circumference. It was such a monster that Mr. Davis concluded to skin and stuff it. While performing the operation he found a Mexican gold coin secreted among its vitals that was used in 1624.

CHAPTER 20
THE CUMBERLAND RIVER MONSTER
"Thrilling Adventure of a Party of Fishermen."

As it is, the state of Tennessee doesn't boast a hearty list of cryptids. It has the Tennessee Wildman, which is a red-haired variety of sasquatch, and even the bizarre Tennessee Red Cheetah, a cryptid ABC (alien big cat).[13] Tennessee has no consistent water monsters to speak of, at least none that have achieved considerable fame. The only one I can find is the obscure "Tennessee Terror" as described in Jason Offutt's *Chasing American Monsters*. According to the tome, the Tennessee River was allegedly the home of a 25 foot serpent first sighted in 1822. The serpentine specter surfaced in front of a farmer out

---

[13] This doesn't mean an extraterrestrial cat, by the way, it just means a big cat outside of its normal environment.

Southerners & Saurians

fishing, and supposedly the fright he suffered later killed him. It made its next appearance in 1827, where a fisherman described it as snake-like and bluish-yellow in color. Today, the legend of the Tennessee Terror has morphed into that of a giant catfish called "Catzilla"—hardly a giant snake.

On April 12, 1868, the *Nashville Union and Dispatch* reported on a traditional looking sea serpent within the Cumberland River of Tennessee. The monster didn't stick around to become a permanent fixture, and similar to the Tennessee Terror, the only "River Monsters" that you'll hear talk of today in the Cumberland are giant catfish.

A CUMBERLAND RIVER MONSTER.
The Great Sea Serpent Supposed to Have Reached Nashville.

Thrilling Adventure of a Party of Fishermen.

They Fire Upon the Monster and Narrowly Escape.

Wondrous things have been recorded of Nashville and the mud dyed Cumberland, but the latest sensation gets beyond anything we remember to have ever heard or read of this mysterious region. The story is certainly marvelous, and we tell it as 'twas told to us, without undertaking to vouch for a thing so strange which we ourself have never seen.

For some six months past, a gentleman living not far from the bank of the river, and about a mile below this city, where a little island lifts itself above the surface of the rapid stream, has been the loser of considerable stock, the cause of the mysterious disappearance of which he until recently has never known. Many a promising pig loosed from the sheltering sty has gone forth for the last time, and all search for its whereabouts proved unavailing. The owner attempted to account for his loss in various ways, and finally concluded that his valuable swine, like those of Holy Writ, had been seized of devils and plunged beneath the sweeping tide near by.

A day or two since, however, the mystery was cleared away. A party of fishermen were out in a boat, taking in a trotline that extended from bank to bank, when they discovered only a short distance from them, an object moving upon the water which they took to be the head of some domestic animal which had taken a notion to swim the river. Their curiosity being somewhat aroused, they approached a little nearer, when to their horror and astonishment a scaly monster, the like of which they had never before seen, slowly raised itself from the water, which fell in a sparkling shower from its body as it rose full six feet above the surface. It appeared to have ears resembling those of a human being, but the head and body were like those of a mammoth serpent.

The party in the boat at once gave chase, and one of them fired several revolver shots at the strange object, but before they could come upon it, they observed a ruffling of the water at a distance of what seemed to their excited imagination to be thirty or forty feet from the body of the monster, and almost instantly a loud splash followed, and a sharp tail like that of a huge snake appeared above the surface, and began thrashing the water furiously as if the wrath of its possessor had been suddenly kindled. The men dropped their oars in blank amazement, but quickly picked them up again as the enraged monster slowly threw its great head and body in the direction of the boat and commenced moving slowly toward them. In the inexpressibly short space of time that a twinkling is supposed to occupy, the boat was partially reversed, and shot out to the shore, where the party landed in safety and put themselves beyond the reach of their terrible pursuer, which, seeing no danger threatened, quietly drew its scaly body beneath the water, and as the ruffled surface became smooth again, the men who stood upon the bank began to doubt the evidence of their senses, so strange was the sight they had so unexpectedly witnessed.

Exactly what sort of a creature the ungainly monster could have been, we have little idea. The persons who saw it state that it had some of the characteristics of and a slight resemblance to the whale. Its resemblance to a serpent would indicate its relation to the great sea serpent, about which so much was said and written a number of years ago, and, for aught we know, it is the veritable old "snake" who created such a sensation at the time. "If this be he," he must have come up from the Caribbean sea after a detour of the West Indies, and getting into the Gulf of Mexico, entered the delta of the Mississippi. Thence ascending the Father of Waters to the junction of the Ohio, he must have visited Cincinnati and Louisville, and struck the Cumberland at Paducah, probably following up some steamer with a case of small-pox aboard, in hope of making a lunch from the unfortunate victim, should the victim be heaved over the side.

Since his appearance the other day, he has not again been seen, and it is surmised that he has now gone on toward the Upper Cumberland, and only got above water here to take a first look at the new country he had reached and to prospect upon his chances of making a living in a fresh water region. The disappearance of porkers and other stock in the vicinity where he was seen, would indicate that he has been near Nashville for some time. If any of our up-river readers get a look at him when he visits them, we trust they will immediately forward us an accurate description of this wonderful denizen of the deep, that the excited public may be set at rest as to his identity.

Sources:

Offutt, Jason. *Chasing American Monsters: Over 250 Creatures, Cryptids & Hairy Beasts.* Woodbury, MN: Llewellyn Publications, 2019.

Southerners & Saurians

SOUTHERN SNAIK STORIES
A "Supernatural" Monster

This is yet another of those tantalizing little blurbs that's begging for more information. Unfortunately, I can find no follow-up articles, but I can confirm that Mr. Rufus T. Beachham was a real man who lived from 1847 to 1909 in Georgia. What his adventures with the "supernatural monster" seen in a swamp south of his farm entailed we do not know, but here is the blurb as printed in the *Atlanta Constitution* on August 18, 1882:

> A Supernatural monster has been seen more than once in the swamp below Mr. Rufus T. Beacham's. Dogs and guns have so far proved useless in trying to bring him in.

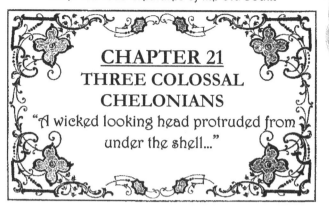

CHAPTER 21
THREE COLOSSAL CHELONIANS
"A wicked looking head protruded from under the shell..."

I n the realm of cryptozoology, there aren't a great many giant turtle cryptids, but there are a few. The most famous of these is Oscar, a giant turtle from Churubusco, Indiana, which caused a brief media furor in the 1940s. In the waters of the South have also been spotted a few colossal chelonians, though. These beasts are infrequent in their appearances and often amount to being one-hit wonders glimpsed but once, never to be seen again. That, or the witnesses killed the beast ending its existence, like this story reported by the *Janesville Gazette* on May 17, 1879:

MONSTER OP THE DEEP.
A Strange Animal Caught Off the Coast of North Carolina.

Southerners & Saurians

From the Wilmington (N. C.) San, There seems to be considerable doubt hanging around what that sea monster shot by Captain Chadwick, of the tug Alpha, on Tuesday last, really is. Some say turtle, some devil-fish, and the Captain himself is of the opinion that it was "Old Nick" himself, and hereafter sinners may have no fear of punishment in the infernal regions. In fact, everybody who hears about it has a different theory, and no two persons can agree on what it is or where it belongs. The Smithville pilots say that his Satanic Majesty has been seen off the coast for the last twenty years, but he has never met any one who was bold enough to attack him until the gallant tug of the Alpha came down on him and put an end to his career. Captain Chadwick sighted the "thing" about eight miles off Western Bar and immediately steered toward it and within a short distance of it he fired at it with his rifle, the ball passing through the neck and killing it. It required six men, with their utmost strength to pull it over the rail, and it is estimated that it weighed six or seven hundred pounds. The animal was seven feet long by three and a half feet wide. On the back was a hard black shell, like a turtle's, with three ridges running lengthwise. The head was as large as a water bucket, and in the mouth, extending down into the throat, were rows of soft teeth. The tail was not more than eighteen inches long, and projected in three prongs. The fins and feet

were like a turtle, with the exception that there
were no claws.

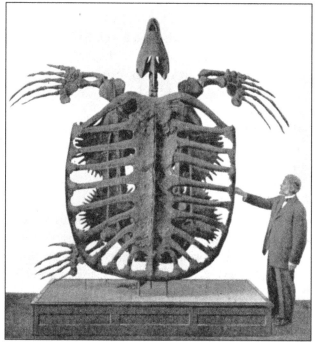

PREHISTORIC ARCHELON SKELETON.

The size of the creature matches that of a
Leatherback Sea Turtle, which can reach a length
of seven feet at its largest. The detail of the teeth is
troubling, though, as no modern turtles possess
teeth, though some prehistoric ones did. The
three-pronged tail is the oddest detail, and doesn't
match any turtle, prehistoric or otherwise, that I
know of.

Moving on, an even bigger turtle monster was
sighted near Cape Sabel in southwestern Florida.

Southerners & Saurians

The story was reported in the *St. Landry Democrat* on November 9, 1889.

A MONSTER TURTLE.

The Cape Sable Advertiser reports that the crew of a fishing schooner a short time since, while a few miles from Cape Sable saw what at first sight they took to be the genuine sea serpent come up to the surface for an airing. They could see the immense black mass was propelling itself slowly away from them, and they resolved on giving chase and having a closer view. The captain and another man sprang into a boat and were soon alongside, when they discovered that it was a turtle of rather vast dimensions, being fully fourteen feet long, eight feet broad, and between five and six feet in thickness. Then a wicked looking head protruded from under the shell to the length of four feet or more. After vain efforts to catch the creature with a gaff, a harpoon was tried, but the iron rebounded from the solid shell, and the attempt had to be abandoned. During the struggle, the monster made the spray fly on all sides and it was not safe to get near him.

Turtles are often seen in this vicinity, and the area is also home to the Everglades National Park, which is one of the most active turtle nesting sites in south Florida. Naturally, nothing like the monster reported here is seen there now, though.

At fourteen feet long, it was twice the size of the other turtle monster story from 1879. It also sounded to have a relatively long neck for a turtle at four feet. So this would sound to be something similar to the group of side-necked turtles known as pelomedusoides. It could have been a Stupendemys, said to reach a maximum length of 11 feet, or better yet, an Archelon which could reach 15 feet.

1914 RESTORATION OF ARCHELON BY SAMUEL WENDELL WILLISTON.

The last significant southern turtle monster story I found appeared ten years later yet again, this time in the *Fort Wayne Sentinel* on July 3, 1899:

CAUGHT A SEA MONSTER.
Creature Weighing Half a Ton Landed In a Fish Net

A peculiar sea monster, weighing half a ton, was caught in a fish net by John A. Smith and his crew while fishing for sturgeon in the Atlantic off Patchogue, L. I, the other day. Smith and his crew had a royal battle in landing the creature.

Southerners & Saurians

Charles Palmer, one of Captain Smith's crew, who has traveled all over the world, says he never saw such a sea monster. It is shaped like a lingo turtle. It is nearly eight feet long, tapering gradually from the junction of the head and spine to the two tails, which spread out on each side. The head is shaped exactly like a tortoise, and the jaws of the large month have an upper and lower set of sawlike teeth, pointing inward. The head is a foot around, and the mouth measures 10 inches. The monster has no feet. It has been embalmed and will be sent to the Central Park Museum of Natural History in New York.—Exchange.

I find this creature interesting because it is similar to the 1879 case, in which the turtle-creature possessed a tail that tapered off into three points, while this one tapered into two. Like that reptile, it also had teeth rather than just a beak. Whatever these chelonian cryptids were, they weren't exclusive to the waters of the South, and giant turtles are glimpsed in waters across the globe.

SOUTHERN SNAIK STORIES
Leviathan of Louisiana

The creature described in the following story resembles nothing currently known in the annals of paleontology. If anything, it sounds made up, and there are no cryptids I'm familiar with that match this description. The story was published in *The Hartford Herald* on December 30, 1914:

A STRANGE CREATURE FOUND IN LOUISIANA.

New Orleans, Dec. 24. - With the head of an elephant, tusks measuring eighteen inches where they enter the mouth, and a body resembling nothing else ever seen to come out of the sea, an eighty-foot monster has been discovered off the southern coast of Louisiana.

The strange creature is dead and dying, partly embedded in sand, off Isle Dernier, a famous resort of the fifties and the scene of Lafcadio Hearn's novel "Chita."

The following telegram was sent to-night by G.J. Labarre and A.M. Dupont, planters of Terrebone Parish, to President Wilson, Congressman Broussard, the Smithsonian Institution and the Louisiana Conservation Commission:

"It is our pleasure to announce as your Christmas greeting that the State of Louisiana has furnished history and science the most wonderful discovery of centuries - the Leviathan of Anthology, eighty feet long, sixteen feet wide, approximately ninety tons weight.

"Description: The head of an elephant, eyes and jaws of the crocodile, the tongue is of a jellylike construction, porous with suckers and shaped like the trunk of an elephant; the tusks protrude in a straight line five feet and are eighteen inches wide at the jaw, and it is apparently a vegetarian."

CHAPTER 22
MONSTER OF THE
MUD VOLCANO
"It's that infernal wog!"

N ear Winder, Georgia, is a boggy pond
called the Nodoroc by the Creek Native
American tribe. Ominously, Nodoroc
translates as the "gateway to hell" in their tongue.
There could be several reasons for this distinction.
Firstly, it is the site of a mud volcano. As the name
implies, a mud volcano is a natural formation that
spews out mud when underground hot water
erupts to the surface. In addition to mud, they also
exude hot gasses, giving them a hellish, volcanic
appearance even though they are not technically
volcanic. A first-hand account of the Nodoroc
appears in G.J.N. Wilson's book *The Early
History of Jackson County*, [Georgia], published in
1914.

A closer inspection revealed the astonishing
fact that the lake was not water, but a body of

three to five acres of smoking, bubbling, bluish mud of about the consistency of molasses, and whose surface ranged from two to three feet below the surrounding solid land. The mud near the banks was slightly in motion, but its action gradually increased towards the center until about half an acre had the appearance of a moderately boiling pot of water. The movement of the smoke which arose from the bubbles was sluggish, and uniting in funnel-shaped form a few feet above the surface, formed the imposing column seen from the distant plain. It was perhaps five feet in diameter at the base, and tapering at the height of at least one-fourth of a mile, spread out like the branches of a tree. Now and then a flickering, bluish blaze, like a flame from a smoldering fire, played for a moment over various parts of the boiling area. This made the smoke more dense than when there was no flame, and the boiling was less violent. It was said by those who had witnessed this uncommon phenomenon on a dark night, that it produced such horrid feelings as to cause some people to faint and made others so sick that they had to be led away. These emotions were probably produced by the unpleasant stench that arose from the lake when the flames were not flickering over it. The fire fed on the ascending gas that was thrown up by the bubbles and thus destroyed the offensive odor.[14]

---

[14] Wilson, *Early History of Jackson County*, pp.146.

MUD VOLCANO IN YELLOWSTONE
NATIONAL PARK C.1912.
LIBRARY OF CONGRESS.

The next reason that the place was called the gateway to hell was its nefarious purpose. The Creek Native American tribe had built a stone altar there where they executed their prisoners. The bodies were then tossed into the bog, or hell. The altar was located on the western shore of the bog, and was a triangular structure twelve feet long and eight feet high.

Southerners & Saurians

There is one other reason for the area's association with hell. Seen in the vicinity is something that could be described as a demon dog or hell hound. It was called the Wog and was first reported in *The Early History of Jackson County.*

Wilson began his section on the Wog writing, "While the wolves, panthers and bears gave the first white settlers of this part of the country much trouble, still another animal whose existence has often been disputed, inspired those who professed to have seen him, with more fear than all the others combined."[15]

The Wog was said to be "a jet-black, long-haired animal about the size of a small horse." The animal was distinct because its legs were shorter than a horse's, and the front legs were longer than the rear by one foot. It was often described as a huge dog "sitting on its tail."[16] Due to its odd legs, when walking, the animal "seemed to require him to carry forward one side at a time."[17] The beast's tail was also very unusual, as it didn't taper to a point, but was bushy and thick all the way through. It was covered in white hair about eight inches long. "Whether sitting, standing or walking this curious appendage was in constant motion from side to side, not as a dog wags his tail, but with a quick upward curve which brought it down with a

---

[15] Ibid, pp.46.
[16] Ibid.
[17] Ibid.

whizzing sound that could be distinctly heard at least when twenty-five or thirty steps distant."[18]

Wilson goes on to say, "But the most distinguishing feature of this horrid tail was that it revealed the presence of the monster in the dark—the only time he ventured to go abroad." Naturally, this monster had glowing red eyes and had an eight-inch long forked tongue uncharacteristic of a mammal. The tongue "played in and out his mouth like those of a mad snake." The head of the beast resembled neither horse nor dog and was said to be bear-like with "a set of great white teeth over which his ugly lips never closed."[19]

GRAINY DEPICTION OF THE WOG.

The first settlers to report the Wog saw it in the vicinity of the old Jug Tavern in 1809. Residents claimed to see it snooping around their homes, and

---

[18] Ibid, pp.46-47.
[19] Ibid, pp.47.

caused no harm despite its horrific appearance. The Creek tribe even told the new settlers that the Wog would do no harm so long as it wasn't disturbed. To keep it from their homes, they were instructed to have a light inside. In this case, the Wog would stick its forked tongue through crevices and openings between the logs, and would then go on its way.

These early day residents never saw the Wog itself, it is reported. Instead, they listened to their animals outside howl and screech in fear. Other than that, they may have heard the whirring of its tail, or seen the forked tongue poke through an opening into their home. Supposedly, the beast didn't harm the animals except for a few that literally died of fright!

The most detailed encounter with the monster came from Alonzo Draper, who told Wilson how it circled his home one night. With him that night was his daughter, Helen, and also a visitor, Abe Trent. Their first warning occurred as they sat outside and their dog began to howl frightfully.

They peered into the distance and spied a pack of wolves. But soon it became evident that the wolves were not the source of their dog's unusual fright. The wolves were themselves frightened of something and began to scatter. They then spied a dark object emerge from the woods. It appeared to be carrying a white flag—really the Wog's strange tail. They watched as the "flag" began to wave and they heard a strange whirring noise.

It was Draper who recognized the creature first, exclaiming, "It's that infernal wog!" Draper had

been taught of the creature by the local Native
Americans, and also knew that it was best to let the
creature pass. Still, Draper was itching to "send a
leaden messenger clean through any part of its
body, or plug one of its fiery eyes out."[20]

Instead, the company decided to take shelter in
the family cabin. They listened from within the
structure to the strange noises the monster made,
and when it came near, it issued a sound similar to
the long-continued hissing of a goose.

True to Wog tradition, it stuck its forked tongue
through an opening in the house. Draper grabbed
his dog before it could bite the tongue and anger
the monster. The Wog circled the house once
more and then made a shout similar to a wild hog.

The family waited in the cabin for some time
before they heard a knock on their door. It was a
neighbor informing them that they had seen the
Wog going away and that they were now all safe.

Shortly after this, the Wog also terrified a
settlement of wigwams at a place called
Haitauthuga. It chased one of the tribe, a man
named Siloquot, up a tree. But thankfully, the
fearsome Wog could not climb because it had
hooves rather than claws.

More accounts of the creature's history came
from the family of Josiah Strong, who had married
the daughter of one of the Creek tribe named
Banna. Her father, Umausauga, was not a chief but
was considered a wise man of importance in the
tribe.

---

[20] Ibid.

Southerners & Saurians

One night, Strong, Banna, and several other families had made camp at Nodoroc. As the party was eating, a woman noticed a foul stench in the air and asked what it was.

"The old wog is getting his breath," said Strong, "as he always does just at noon. Father Umausauga warned me of this, but I had forgotten to mention it."[21]

At the behest of the curious group, Umausauga came and gave a history of the Nodoroc, beginning,

To the mind of the Creek Indian Nodoroc means about the same as hell does to the white man, and Wog corresponds to devil, or Satan. For the meaning and application of these names I am indebted to my darling Banna, and I have full faith in all that she says. I was myself once so much afraid of the wog-devil that I sold the land on which he mostly traveled, and only a few of my race will live on it. The Creeks believe that all bad spirits are sent here and when their bodies die and sometimes they die here and the wog smooths over the hole they make when entering the mud by sweeping his ugly tail from side to tide.[22]

Umausauga continued,

A long time ago the place was hotter than it is now. Even when I was a boy you could

---

[21] Ibid, pp.148-149.
[22] Ibid.

sometimes see solid sheets of flame shooting over the surface like lightning in a southern storm-cloud; and the boiling mud would pop and crack like a burning canebrake. All this made people, and its present condition still makes some people believe, that the wog was mad because enough bad spirits were not sent to him. This belief caused innocent victims to be thrown into the horrid place to satisfy revengeful and overbearing natures and to keep the wog from visiting them at night.[23]

Obviously, the Wog's rather unearthly description reeks of folklore. If the creature was a real animal, the closest thing it could've resembled was a vicious ice age mammal, perhaps an extinct "bear dog" or Sarkastodon. But if one leans towards the supernatural, and it really was a variety of hell hound, then there could be another explanation. Perhaps the Wog vanished once no more sacrifices were made at Nodoroc?

Another big problem with the Wog is that it is rarely seen today. The only post 1900-era sighting I found came courtesy of the 109th episode of *30 Odd Minutes* entitled "Your Cryptid Encounters." Brandon Parker from Fort Bennings, Georgia, saw the creature in the summer of 2012 while doing PT with his troupe. Parker was running alone when he saw what he thought was a hog sitting on the side of the road. He eventually began to notice that it had some notable differences from a hog, beginning

---

[23] Ibid, pp.149-150.

with a long bushy tail and an exceptionally muscular chest region. It sat as high as a Great Dane and had a dog's face but with a hog's ears and characteristics. The creature looked at him and took a step forward and Parker ceased his viewing and decided to make tracks.

Parker told his wife about his encounter, and she told him that his description sounded like that given to the Georgia Wog. The show's host then showed Parker a drawing of the Wog, which Parker agreed looked very similar to the creature that he saw.[24]

In summary, though not well known, there seems to be a decent amount of testimony vouching for the Wog's existence. What it is, exactly, can hopefully be determined upon further investigation.

Sources:

G.J.N. *The Early History of Jackson County.* Atlanta, GA: Atlanta, Foote and Davies co., 1914.

"Your Cryptid Encounters." *30 Odd Minutes.* (YouTube series) [https://www.youtube.com/watch?v=E7rbMXuV2HU]

---

[24] After this, another member of the show brought up the possibility that it was a member of the Shunka Warak'in species. The Shunka Warak'in is a proven cryptid with physical evidence in the form of a taxidermied body currently on display in the Madison Valley History Museum.

POSTSCRIPT

DINOSAURUS OF THE EVERGLADES

When I first read this story a few years ago it had me quite excited. It tells of a hunter in the Everglades killing some sort of dinosaur. My first skeptical thought was that the tale might have been influenced by Sir Arthur Conan Doyle's *The Lost World*. However, Doyle's classic novel was published in 1912, and this article was printed in 1901. I found this to be quite encouraging.

Of course, there had been plenty of articles published by this time that claimed to tell of men killing prehistoric beasts. That wasn't what intrigued me. What fascinated me was just how far ahead of its time the piece was as it seemed to describe what we would today call cryptozoologists.

The term cryptozoology wasn't coined until the late 1950s. During that decade, Bernard

177

Southerners & Saurians

Heuvelmans had published *On the Track of Unknown Animals*. He defined his studies as cryptozoology based off of three Greek words: *kryptos* (hidden), *zoon* (animals), *logos* (discourse). Over the next thirty years, the concept of cryptozoology would continue to develop and evolve until the International Society of Cryptozoology was founded in 1982.

The article from 1901 would seem to describe early 20th Century cryptozoologists in the form of a "secret society" of scientists out to prove that dinosaurs survived into the modern era. What really struck me was the way that the article addressed the Smithsonian Institute. By now, you have probably noticed that most of these old articles conclude by stating that a carcass or a piece of flesh of some mysterious animal will be sent to the Smithsonian. Of course, if that were the case, where are these amazing artifacts today? Were they lost in the mail? Were they made up to begin with? Or, is a conspiracy afoot?

Several—but not all—of today's cryptozoologists and Fortean researchers believe that the Smithsonian Institute covers up the existence of prehistoric survivors much in the same way that the military tried for many years to deny the existence of UFOs and extraterrestrials.

This is the only article from antiquity that I have seen thus far to make the comment that the "artifact" (i.e., the dead dinosaur) will not make its way to the Smithsonian due to an alleged cover-up. This is also one of the earliest articles to postulate that dragon legends came from surviving dinosaurs, another common facet of cryptozoology today.

However, there are quite a few things wrong with this article,[25] which we will discuss after you have finished reading it for yourself:

STRANGE STILL-HUNT BY SCIENTISTS REVEALED BY KILLING OF A DINOSAURS

Search for a Reptile Commonly Believed to Be Extinct Rewarded in the Florida Everglades.

In the thick, steamy depths of the Everglades of Florida there has just been killed a reptile which upsets tradition, plays havoc with the theories of geologists and confounds the lore of the paleontologists. A hunter of today has sent a modern bullet through the skull of a creature which, according to science, should have been dead ten thousand years ago. He has killed a Dinosaurus, one of the gigantic, prehistoric, flesh-eating lizards, whose fossil bones men have been accustomed to inspect reverently in museums.

The last shot which echoed around the world was a cannon shot, and it moved nations; this was but the crack of a magazine rifle, but it has stirred the world as no mere war could do, for

---

[25] I regret to say I have misplaced the exact date and paper that I got my version of the story from. But, the earliest variation of the story that I can find was published December 1, 1901, in the *New York Times*.

that hunter's bullet has practically overthrown science itself and pierced the vitals of geological knowledge.

There is no doubt of the identity of the creature which has been shot in Florida's Everglades. It is a Dinosaurus, a species of gigantic reptile whose bones alone sometimes weigh ten tons. The specimen shot in Florida is of medium size, but it is still stupendous. Its exact measurement has not yet been obtained for reasons which will presently be explained, but the ordinary size of a Dinosaurus is 35 feet.

Only part of the tale has been told, however, when it is said that a living Dinosaurus has been shot in the Everglades of Florida. The most interesting part of the story, indeed, is only known to those who understand the inner facts—to those few who know that the discovery and the death of the Dinosaurus was no mere accident, but the direct result of a carefully conducted search for living prehistoric animals which for a long time has been systematically pursued by a thoroughly equipped society of scientists.

According to the story which has been allowed to reach the public, a hunter in the Everglades noticed a tremendous track through the swamp grasses which he thought had been made by a mammoth alligator. For several days he tried to track the supposed alligator, but failing to do so he at last climbed a tree by the side of the tracks and waited there for two days.

At last he saw what seemed to him to be an immense serpent approaching through the marsh. Then he saw that the thing had legs, that it was more than fifty feet long and as big, in its thickest part, as a hogshead. When it got near to him he was astonished to see it raise its head until it was almost on a level with his own face. He saw that it looked like a gigantic reptilian kangaroo.

Then, says the story, the man shot at its head and hit it. The thing sought to escape and the hunter fired at it as it ran until his magazine was empty. He was using bullets which would penetrate iron plate. He did not try to follow it as he was too much alarmed by the reptile's proportions.

Several days later, so the story continues, the hunter saw a great cloud of vultures and went to see what they were devouring. He found the body of the creature he had shot at, but it was so badly torn by birds and animals that he was only able to secure its head. The skeleton, it is added, is to be sent to the Smithsonian Museum.

"That skeleton will never reach the museum," said a man whose devoted and single minded pursuit of science has taken all of his time and most of his fortune. "I am surprised that the society has allowed the matter to become public, as it has further work to do in the Everglades. However, since the story is out, and since much good and no harm can be done by a quiet discussion of the truth of this surprising matter, I will give you the history of the entire matter if you will respect my desire to remain unknown.

"Paleontologists and those other allied scientists who make a particular study of the osteology of prehistoric vertebrates, have long had excellent reasons for entertaining the belief that not all the gigantic reptiles and animals of the past have entered into the fossil state. Traditionally, the last of these animals and reptiles passed away at the time nature was beginning to manufacture our present supply of coal, but in actual fact the time of their death—often in the majority of cases—can be placed very much later.

"Anthropologists, too, long ago pointed out that the legends and folklore tales of dragons, griffins and monstrous lizards had their probable origin in actual fact, and were no mere figments of fancy. The tales of dragons and griffins, they say, were really accounts, garbled in long transmission, of real, live things. Any one of the great lizards whose bones are now found in the earth, would have made a real dragon of antiquity. The great flying beasts which scientists call Pterodactyls, were probably the originals of the flying griffins of tradition, and, in the same way, all the other reptiles and animals of what we call "fable" had their actual origin in fact.

"Since it is necessarily true that the days of traditions very nearly join hands with the days of fact, several scientists who are possessed of rather more imagination than their fellows have quietly considered the possibility of some of these animals being still alive. According to the rocks, the Dinosaurs, the Brontosaurs and the Pterodactyls, passed into stone several thousand years ago. In the same way orthodox science declares that the Mammoth has been extinct for centuries and that all the other creatures of that day have passed away. Science deals with fact, it says, and frowns upon imagination. Geological periods show that the creatures of other days could not live under present conditions, say the stricter scientists, and they are accustomed to regard with mingled amusement and anger those who would even notice a theory which admits the possibility of an "extinct" animal being found alive.

"In spite of this ridicule there has nevertheless long existed a small group of scientists who seek persistently for evidences that 'extinct' monsters had possessed life up to much more recent times than geologists generally believed. These men observed that most of the legends of dragons, griffins and gigantic reptiles seemed to have flourished during the days of ancient chivalry. Knights in armor seemed to go naturally with dragons and other supposedly mythical beasts, and while antiquity furnished them with some such traditional beasts as the Minotaur and Centaurs the best and most circumstantial of the 'dragon' tales centered around the 'Age of Chivalry.'

183

Southerners & Saurians

"There seemed to be a good reason for this, for it was during the period of Knight errantry that the world was really explored. Knights in armor, with their squires and followers, seem to have penetrated to the most unlikely places, and while they seem to have religiously refrained from the exploration of cold countries they were not deterred, apparently, by any degree of heat, whether moist or dry.

"Reptiles such as the dinosaurus lived in an age when the earth's atmosphere was that of the steam room of a Turkish bath and when rank, dense vegetation grew upon every side. Amphibious, they passed their lives in the tepid waters and upon the marshy, densely shaded portions of land which then formed the North American continent. In every place in which the skeletons or fossilized remains of these great reptiles have been discovered geologists found that these two conditions of moist heat and dense vegetation had been present.

"By careful research into the rocks and the geography of the country surrounding the places in which these fossil remains were found, this little group of advanced but ridiculed scientists were able to describe with a great deal of accuracy the exact climate and geographical conditions which were necessary to the existence of these enormous reptiles. Later they extended their researches to the extinct mammals and were able to describe the sort of country and the kind of climate in which the mammoth used to flourish. From this data, and

that with which they were readily furnished by
the scientists of the various governments, these
men were able to prepare a map which showed
those districts in which the climatic and
geographical conditions of the present
corresponded with those once enjoyed by the
gigantic animals of other days.

"North America—especially the Wyoming
territory—is so rich in the fossil remains of
extinct animals and reptiles that it has been
called the graveyard of the old world. For this
reason these few hopeful scientists paid
particular attention to the United States. They
did not know if it would ever be given to them
to prove that not all the ancient animals were
dead, but they firmly believed that they were
more likely to find live specimens in the United
States than anywhere else in the world.

"Necessarily the districts of which there was a
remote possibility of the survival of one of these
monstrous beasts were not very many. The
requisites were that the climate should be like
that of ancient times, and that the country itself
should be utterly forsaken and impassable to
man.

"In all the United States there seemed to be
but two places which even began to fulfill these
conditions—the Dismal Swamp, between
Virginia and North Carolina, and the
Everglades, in the southern extremity of
Florida. Of these two places the Everglades
alone seemed a probable place. The Dismal

Southerners & Saurians

Swamp, although fulfilling some of the conditions set forth by the scientists, has been so encroached upon by hunters and surveyors that hardly a mile of its thirty-five remained unexplored. In earlier days it might well have been the last retreat of some of the prehistoric animals, but no one would nowadays expect to find anything but the remains of such animals in the Dismal Swamp.

"There remained, then, only the Everglades, an extensive marshy region in southern Florida, consisting, practically, of a great shallow lake, in which are many low islands, varying in size from a few square yards to hundreds of acres, and covered with a dense jungle of pines, palmettos, vines and tropical trees. The water between the islands is from one to six feet deep, and is covered with tall, feathery grass which grows from the bottom and gives the whole region a most beautiful appearance. Lying within the tropics, the shallowness of the water, the density of the vegetation and the steady heat of the sun make of the region a country of steady moisture, exactly resembling, as far as the science of today can judge, the conditions under which the great mammals and reptiles of the past ages existed.

"It would be difficult probably to think of anything more chimerical than a hunt having for its object the discovery of living specimens of 'extinct' monsters, and yet this is the sort of search which has been deliberately undertaken by a number of hard-headed scientists during the last five years. Dreading publicity and ridicule, alike, the search has been conducted with the greatest secrecy under the guise of an attempt to classify fauna and flora of the region. It has never flagged European or Asiatic scientists would have been discouraged long ago, but the Americans who undertake the work either knew too much or too little to be willing to relinquish the quest.

"They knew, for instance, that in several parts of the United States there still existed things which in other countries had been reduced to fossils. The giant trees of California, for instance, the Sequoia, are the same sort of trees under which the mammoth disported himself when the world was young. These trees, undisturbed until man came, not only exist, but still flourish under almost the same conditions that supported the mammoth, the pterodactyl and the dinosaurus. They knew, too, that several times, in the north, remains of the mammoth had been discovered amid circumstances which showed that the gigantic animal had been alive within a few years. Aware that the publication of such a statement concerning mammoths would bring down upon them a storm of ridicule, the scientists kept such discoveries as this to themselves. It is no light thing to attempt to overthrow the cherished theories and creeds of the geologists, paleontologists and other scientists. The men who found these mammoth remains knew that it was quite useless to attempt to make any of the orthodox scientists believe that such animals could have existed within, recent times. Officially, the last mammoth died ten thousand years ago, and a living mammoth would be an anachronism—an utter impossibility—which no self-respecting paleontologist would tolerate. The discoverers felt sure that even if an orthodox scientist met a mammoth face to face he would refuse to believe in its existence and would promptly endeavor to demonstrate its chimerical character.

"For this reason—and several other reasons of equal weight—the seekers for living prehistoric animals have preserved rigid secrecy concerning their search. Fortunately, several rich men have become personally interested in the work and these have given not only their money, but their time to the cause. Several tentative attempts were made to gain the attention of the orthodox faction among geologists, but every attempt of the kind met with laughter and sneers until finally the searchers, secure in the possession of their own knowledge, gave up all attempts to convert the heathen.

"The men interested in the search were thoroughly convinced that careful investigation would show that a few of the animals and reptiles hitherto supposed to be extinct had nevertheless survived through the ages. They believed that in the depths of the sea and in the great unsounded abysses of the southern oceans there yet remained living specimens of the marine creatures that lived in other days. They believed that in certain specially favored and secluded corners of the earth there yet existed living descendants of the colossal monsters which once ravaged the earth, but they thoroughly appreciated the fact that they would experience great difficulty in getting any one to believe it.

"It seemed to them, in fact, that there was but one way in which their position could be made plain; but one way in which the other skeptical scientists could be made to see that the society had not been chasing a myth. They must produce either a living specimen, or one so recently dead that there would be no room for doubt as to its having been alive within the year. It was a bold plan—an impossible one, it seemed—for it meant the patient searching of every foot of the ground in those few places in which such creatures could still live.

"Then came the discovery and the slaughter of the first mammoth found living in the present age.

"It has long been the practice of the society to investigate the strange tales brought by hunters and travelers concerning monstrous animals. Whenever hunters, explorers or prospectors brought back to the towns stories of gigantic beasts or reptiles they were sure to be approached, sooner or later, by some quiet, unassuming man who seemed to possess a strange talent for asking questions and a wonderful knack of drawing. Usually, too, he had with him some pictures of strange beasts, which he would show to the hunter as he talked. Always, in the beginning, the visitor would persuade the hunter, explorer or prospector to tell his story. He would listen most patiently and make sure of the locality. Then he would rapidly draw a strange looking animal and ask the hunter whether the animal he had seen looked anything like the sketch. It was very seldom, indeed, that it did. Picture after picture was usually drawn and rejected and then books would be brought out, but it was not very often that the man with the story was able to bring joy to our man with the quest.

"The man who asked questions and drew pictures was one of our emissaries—or often one of the members—of the little group of scientists I have told you of who believe in the existence of living monsters. They investigated every story they heard, rejecting unerringly those which were manifestly impossible, as well as those which hailed from unlikely parts of the world.

"Once there came down to one of the cities a man who had heard a story from an Indian — who had it from an Alaskan, who had it, in his turn, from no one knew who. It was the story of a gigantic animal with great, curving tusks, a tremendous trunk and a vast body covered with shaggy wool and hair. The Alaskan had identified it without trouble. Since his boyhood he had made a living by gathering the tusks of frozen mammoths and he had told the Indian that there was in the northland a live animal which bore tusks like those he had gathered.

The society heard of the tale; they followed it up. Then at last they sent east a telegram which brought all the resources and skill of the little company of scientists to the solution of that one problem.

"Somewhere, on the borders of Siberia, they believed there existed a living mammoth.

"They found it at last, this great towering, shaggy, terrifying beast. Two men's lives it cost in the first reconnoitering stamping them into a ruddy, shapeless pulp beneath feet that in very fact made the earth shake. It had slain scores of men, said the guides, charging always upon them when they lay by their camp fires.

From that hint there was formed a plan. The scientists believed that the only thing feared by this monster, in the land of ice, volcanoes and geysers, was fire. They thought that it charged upon the camps to extinguish the fires which it felt endangered the peaty bogs and deep, semi-Arctic mosses of its home, and that its annihilation of the accompanying human beings was unnoticed.

They tried, by a ruse, to discover the truth. Three large piles of brushwood were made a mile apart, and, by a device, they were fired simultaneously. From crevices in the rocks they watched the thing which had outlived its age rush upon the first fire and toss aside the brushwood with its tusks before it trampled out the brands. Thence it circled to the next fire, and to the next. The last was burning brightly and fiercely, but it was attacked without hesitation, and extinguished amid terrifying trumpetings and screams of pain.

Around the eighty-foot stump of a gigantic tree a ring of brushwood was made. Without that there was built another ring, and then another, the first being a hundred feet distant from the base of the tree. Upon a platform, in the tree, three men, who were sharpshooters, took their station. They were armed with specially made rifles, firing a steel-tipped bullet that would penetrate four inches of wrought iron. The rifles fired a projectile that was practically an explosive shell, bursting within and rending horribly the carcass of any animal they struck. Ordinarily elephants fell before them at one shot, like rabbits.

"The men who climbed into the tree with a hundred rounds of shells apiece knew that they had not one chance in a thousand of descending alive, but the pursuit of science demands these sacrifices. They took their places, and from a long distance, by electricity, the outer ring of brushwood, saturated with oil, was set alight. Hardly had it blazed up when the monster rushed from the place where none had dared to follow, and attacked the fire. Each man had been assigned to fire at a particular spot, and no bullet was to be wasted.

"A hail of explosive bullets fell upon the gigantic beast. He saw nothing but the fire; fought nothing but the fire. Blood poured from him as he scattered the second ring of flames, and still the steady, machine-like rattle of the magazine rifles continued.

"Not until a hundred bullets had been fired into his carcass did the mammoth seem to know that the hurts he received came from anything but his ancient foe, the fire. Then he raised his head, and seemed to see the men. Trumpeting so that even these men were terrified, he dashed through the fire to the tree, and struck it with his tusks. Thick as the thickest oak, and rooted in rock, the tree, nevertheless, quivered, groaned and cracked. Nothing but the ropes which bound the men in place saved them, and, as it was, one of them lost his rifle from the shock.

"From head, shoulders, and body poured the life of the shattered monster as he drew back to make another charge that should bring down the tree. Firing desperately for their lives the marksmen aimed for the mammoth's eyes, and, blinded, the great beast seemed to hesitate. Then gradually, tremendously, as a hill engulfed by an earthquake might sink, the mountainous brute sank to the ground. The steel clad shells of the modern rifle had done their work upon this monstrous relic of the dead ages.

"How the torn skin was removed from that shattered carcass, how the flesh was saved and the body dissected, examined, compared, measured and photographed are part of the secret archives of the society. The men who did the work were satisfied with the result of their expedition, even if the rest of the scientific world was not. A quiet attempt was made to see if the orthodox would, under any circumstances, admit the possibility of the existence of a prehistoric mammoth at the present day. It was found that the orthodox would believe no such thing and that, having received some hint of the matter, they were prepared to cry 'fraud' and to cast doubt upon the matter. The skin, said these, could have been obtained from a glacier. The injuries might have been made after death, they hinted. Even the fresh blood, with its curious nucleated corpuscles, might have been drawn from a frozen body—and, in fact, it seemed to be quite easy for the orthodox to prove, even, that the mammoth had been manufactured from a dead elephant and a few miscellaneous animals.

"For this reason we abandoned all attempts to make public the facts of the killing of the mammoth. A later age, with better knowledge and the faith which comes of learning, will be told of the death of the monster that had outlived its age, and it will believe in the anachronism, because it will be able to place beside the statements the other facts and the other prehistoric but living animals which are yet to be found by the seekers of our society.

"One of them will be the dinosaurus, shot by our men in the Everglades of Florida."

Oddly enough, it's not the dead dinosaur that kills this story. It's the mammoth. Back in October of 1899, *McClure's Magazine* published a fictional story on the killing of a mammoth in then-modern-day Alaska. It was titled "The Killing of the Mammoth" and was even identified as fiction in the magazine's table of contents. However, it was written so convincingly that almost everyone who read it thought it was real. Later, the magazine had to publish the following disclaimer:

"The Killing of the Mammoth" by H. Tukeman was printed purely as fiction, with no idea of misleading the public, and was entitled a story in our table of contents. We doubt if any writer of realistic fiction ever had a more general and convincing proof of success.

The 1901 article came just two years on the heels of the Mammoth story by Tukeman. Though the 1901 article's version of the tale has some slight variations, it was clearly meant to be the same story. I had to ponder whether or not that the article's writer was among the deceived. Perhaps they thought the *McClure's Magazine* story was real like so many others. However, I think the writer was himself among the deceivers. Upon closer examination, the story of the killing of the dinosaur in the Everglades is itself incredibly similar to "The Killing of the Mammoth" in that a hunter lies in wait for his prehistoric prey in a tree. He blasts it full of lead, but finds the body too large to take in one piece, and has to settle for slicing off pieces to send to the Smithsonian. You see, even though it was a work of fiction, the "Killing of the Mammoth" also ended by stating that the remains were given to the Smithsonian.

Southerners & Saurians

A more detailed version of the Everglades dinosaur story (with even more similarities to the mammoth tale) was printed in the *Republican News Item* on February 13, 1902.

STRANGE MONSTER IN FLORIDA.
Reptile Formerly Thought to Be a Creature of Indian Imagination.

An enormous reptile, more like the extinct brontosaurus, or fabled sea-serpent than any living creature, has just been killed by a hunter in the lower Florida Everglades. He means to send the skeleton to the Smithsonian Institution at Washington.

"Dragon of the Everglades," from a Sketch by an Indian.

It has for 100 years not only been a tradition among the Seminole Indians who inhabited the borders of Lake Okeechobee, but it is stated as a fact within the knowledge of some of the Indians now living that an immense serpent made its home in the Everglades and has carried off at least two Indians.

The Indians reported the animal to be snakelike in appearance, with ears like a deer; that it had only been seen in the Everglades, and that it was very wild. They said that when it traveled it frequently stopped, raised its head high above the sawgrass to take a view of its surroundings to discover enemies or to locate victims, a deer, bear, hog, or some other animal. If frightened, the Indians asserted that it glided off at immense speed.

These stories have kept the venturesome hunter and trapper on his guard and in a state of more or less anxiety, notwithstanding they did not give credence to these Indian stories. Recently Buster Ferrel, one of the boldest and most noted of the hunters of Okeechobee, who for 20 years has made the border of the lake and the Everglades his home on one of his periodical expeditions noted what he supposed to be the pathway of an immense alligator.

For several days he visited the locality with the hope of killing the saurian but was unsuccessful in finding him. His pride as a hunter was piqued, and his desire to obtain the hide of what he felt sure to be one of the largest alligators ever seen in this section, where alligators are noted for their immense size, grew daily. He studied some plan to outwit it. A large cypress stood near its pathway, and he concluded to climb the tree and take a stand for his game. He accordingly took his position in the tree. For two days, he stood watch with his rifle ready. Nothing appeared. He was becoming discouraged but determined to give one more day to the effort.

On the third day, before he had been on his perch an hour, he saw what looked to him like an immense serpent gliding along the supposed alligator track. He estimated it to be anywhere from 25 to 30 feet long and fully 10 to 12 inches in diameter where the head joined the body and as large around as a barrel 10 feet further back. The creature stopped within easy range of his gun and raised high its head. As it did Ferrel shot at its head. Taken by surprise the serpent dashed into the marsh at tremendous speed, while Ferrel kept up firing until he had emptied the magazine of his rifle.

About four days afterward he ventured back into the neighborhood and about a mile from where he first saw the monster he saw a large flock of buzzards, and went to see what they were after, and there he found the creature dead, and its body so badly torn by the buzzards that it was impossible to save the skin.

He, however, secured the head, and has it now in his home on the Kissimmee river. It is truly a frightful looking object, fully 10 inches from jaw to jaw, and ugly, razor-like teeth. He described the animal as dark colored on its back and a dingy white beneath, with feelers around its mouth similar to a catfish.

He has gone back into the swamp with the intention of obtaining the skeleton and bringing it back, after which he will send it to the Smithsonian Institution in Washington.

To hammer in the final nails in this story's coffin, let's start with some inconsistencies. Illustrations of the monster present it as though it's a Chinese dragon, while the witnesses account makes it sound more like a brontosaurus or an iguanodon. Another red flag is the witness describing the creature as being like a reptilian kangaroo in the previous article. At the time, it was in vogue to compare bipedal dinosaurs to kangaroos. Paleontologists of the time even felt the animals might hop like kangaroos, though this has since been disproven.

Though the monster may or may not have been real, Buster Ferrel did at least exist. Historical records refer to him in the *Kissimmee Valley Gazette* from April 22, 1898:

A man by the name of Davis that was cut by Arthur Speer of Orange county some time ago died at Buster Ferrel's camp on Okeechobee beach last week of blood poison caused from a deep gash under his shoulder blade. I guess spear cut deeper than he meant.

Though articles like these are always exciting upon first glance, upon deeper examination, they ultimately prove disappointing for crypto-zoologists. However, dubious stories like these by no means debunk cryptid sightings from reliable witnesses. Nor do they ruin the credibility of other articles that might be genuine, though they certainly do hurt them.

Based upon the heaps of evidence and credible sightings the world over, I still have no doubt that brontosaurs roam the Likouala Swamp of Africa and that Sasquatch stride through the Pacific

Northwest on a regular basis. To a lesser degree, I think a few Lizardmen might even haunt the swamps of the South along with a few river serpents and Wogs. But as for the Gallinippers, Sea Devils, and Dinosauruses of the Everglades, they make for some fun folklore, but at the end of the day, that's most likely all that they are.

All that said, keep watching those swamps, just in case...

INDEX

ABOUT THE AUTHOR

John LeMay was born and raised in Roswell, New Mexico, famous for its 1947 UFO crash. He is a historian who has written over twenty books, most of them on Southwestern history such as *Tall Tales and Half Truths of Billy the Kid*. He is the co-author/co-creator of *The Real Cowboys and Aliens* series with Noe Torres. Like the *Cowboys & Saurians* series, *The Real Cowboys and Aliens* explores UFO sightings and alien encounters of the Pioneer Period. LeMay is also a past president of the Historical Society for Southeast New Mexico and has written for magazines such as *Cinema Retro, True West, G-Fan, Mad Scientist* and *Xenorama*. LeMay also writes film histories such as *Kong Unmade: The Lost Films of Skull Island* and is the editor and publisher of *The Lost Films Fanzine*.

Also Available

This book has a counterpart for young readers, *Monsters of the Old South*, containing the same tales of Lizardmen, dinosaurs, and swamp monsters, only adapted for readers aged 9-12.

120 pages/$12.99

Made in the USA
Monee, IL
09 June 2024

59614307R00115